CHANGING PERCEPTION OF FREEDOM

Changing Perception of Freedom

Civil Society and Its Response to United Liberation Front of Asom

Prateeti Barman

AKANSHA PUBLISHING HOUSE
New Delhi • Guwahati • Visakhapatnam

AKANSHA PUBLISHING HOUSE
4649/21-B, Ansari Road
Daryaganj, New Delhi - 110 002
E-mail: ektabooks@yahoo.com
Phones: 011-23263193, 09435116718
visit us: www.akanshapublishinghouse.com

Changing Perception of Freedom

First Published, 2010

ISBN 978-81-8370-244-7

PRINTED IN INDIA

Published by Akansha Publishing House, New Delhi - 2 and Printed at Harmain Offset Printers, Delhi.

Contents

Contents

Foreword

This book has been a result of a project carried out by Prateeti when we were working as a part of the Peace Studies team, in Omeo Kumar Das Institute of Social Change and Development in Assam. We were interested in finding out how an insurgent group like ULFA (United Liberation Front of Asom) continued to get the popular support after committing heinous crime like killing innocent children. We had come across bureaucrats, teachers, students still having faith in the insurgent group. In some other parts of northeastern region like Nagaland, Manipur or NC Hills of Assam, support of this section of people seem to be making things easier for these groups. We were interested in finding out the reasons behind this support. Prateeti did a detailed field study to analyze the situation, met people belonging to the insurgent groups as well as different sections of the civil society. Thus she was able to collect some information which was helpful to understand the problem. Though there are few books on ULFA, nobody has discussed this issue particularly the relationship of ULFA with the civil society organization of Assam.

In order to do the study two areas were selected which had the record of producing highest number of youths who had become members of this insurgent groups-Nalbari and Tinsukia districts besides Dibrugarh and Guwahati. Interviewing the various sections of civil society, the researcher found a major group of civil society members, womenfolk of these districts in particular still refer to the members of this insurgent groups as 'our boys'. These villagers specially women & girls faced a lot of problem in the hands of the military and paramilitary forces when search was going on.

With the objective of bringing about peace in the region, Peace Studies took up means like bringing group of insurgents who were on ceasefire to dialogue with different members of the society. Research is another important instrument of doing an empirical study. Why did a bunch of young boys and girls took up arms against the state? In course of their long movement they have changed their nature of activities. Once committed to the social cause the insurgent group has carried on number of extortion, kidnapping, killing, explosions etc.

It is interesting to note that there is factionalism growing within the organization. The state has developed policies to weaken the origination. There are groups who are on ceasefire yet ULFA is continuing its activities. The question was what were the sources which were actually helping ULFA to survive?

Prateeti has done a good work meeting some members of the insurgent groups, their family members, victims, neighbors etc. A number of people have helped us in this effort. This is a first book of the young scholar. I hope intellectuals will help her in carrying out future research by offering constructive criticism.

—Anuradha Dutta

Acknowledgements

The study on Changing Perception of Freedom: Civil Society and Its Response to United Liberation Front of Asom is the outcome of one and half years journey in various parts of Assam. This emotional as well as probing journey would not have been possible without the unconditional help from the people concerned.

I am thankful to our Director Prof. Indranee Dutta for her encouragement. I am indebted to Prof. Anuradha Dutta, Chair, Peace Studies for her guidance and support. She was always there for me in every step of the study with her emotional support, suggestions, and relevant materials. I would also like to thank Prof. A.N.S Ahmed and Dr. Samir Kr. Das for their invaluable comments during and after the study.

I am grateful to Abhijit Neog, Pranab Phukan, Parag Bhuyan, Manas Dutta, Brojen Choudhury and Faizur Rahman without whom this study would have been impossible. They took out time from their busy schedule to take me to the interior fields. I would also like to thank my colleagues Afruza, Jahnabi and Urmimala for their help in various stages of the study. A special thanks to my husband Arnob for designing the cover of the book and the maps. I would like to appreciate the help I received from our Librarian G.B. Devchoudhury and Rustam Ali for the statistical help. I am thankful to my parents who offered their constant support throughout the journey. Last but not the least I would like to extend my heartfelt gratitude to my participants without whom this study would not have been possible.

Prateeti Barman

Glossary of Terms

AASU	All Assam Student's Union
AFSPA	Armed Forces (Special Powers) Act
AGP	Asom Gana Parishad
AJYCP	Asom Jatiyotabadi Yuva Chatra Parishad
APLA	Assam People Liberation Army
ATTF	All-Tripura Tribal Force
CPI	Communist Party of India
CS	Civil Society
DFI	Defense Forces Intelligence
DGFI	Directorate General of Field Intelligence
DHD	Dima Halam/Halim Daogah
ISI	Inter Services Intelligence
KIA	Kachin Independence Army
MNF	Mizo National Front
NDFB	National Democratic Front of Bodoland
NLTF	National Liberation Front of Tripura
NMA	Naga Mothers Association
NSCN	National Socialist Council of Nagaland
NSCN-IM	National Socialist Council of Nagalim-Isak-

	Muivah faction
NSCN-K	National Socialist Council of Nagalim-Khaplang faction
PLA	People's Liberation Army
RCPI	Revolutionary Communist Party of India
RGM	Revolutionary Government of Manipur
TAGS	Tamulpur Anchalik Gramdan Sangh
TNV	Tripura National Volunteers
ULFA	United Liberation Front of Asom
UNLF	United National Liberation Front
UPDS	United Peoples' Democratic Solidarity

1

Insurgency

Over the years, the world has seen terror attacks in different parts of it. Especially in the last ten years, terrorism has taken a more violent form; the most recent one can be 9/11 in the United States of America. Before 9/11, though there were instances of terrorist attacks, however, those did not gather that much of an importance. In fact, growing number of terrorist organizations are coming up every day. Terrorism has affected the innocent civilians all over the world. The act of terrorism has almost replaced traditional warfare, which is declared and has a defined objective. Terrorism is, on the other hand, an undeclared war through which terrorists try to realize their objectives. It is very difficult to define the term 'terrorism'. There are one hundred definitions on 'terrorism' listed in a book titled "Political Terrorism" by Alex Schmid, 1983.[1] According to Martha Crenshaw, Department of Government, Wesleyan University:

> "The problem of defining terrorism has hindered analysis since the inception of studies of terrorism in the early 1970s. One set of problems is due to the fact that the concept of terrorism is deeply contested. The use of the term is often polemical and rhetorical. It can be a pejorative label, meant to condemn an opponent's cause as illegitimate rather than describe behavior. Moreover, even if the term is used objectively as an analytical tool, it is still difficult to arrive at a satisfactory definition that distinguishes terrorism from other violent phenomena. In principle, terrorism is deliberate and

systematic violence performed by small numbers of people, whereas communal violence is spontaneous, sporadic, and requires mass participation. The purpose of terrorism is to intimidate a watching popular audience by harming only a few, whereas genocide is the elimination of entire communities. Terrorism is meant to hurt, not to destroy.

Terrorism is preeminently political and symbolic, whereas guerrilla warfare is a military activity. Repressive "terror" from above is the action of those in power, whereas terrorism is a clandestine resistance to authority. Yet in practice, events cannot always be precisely categorized."[2]

The Psychology of Terrorism: An Agenda for the 21st Century, Terrorism has caused unmitigated unrest in this world and has affected adversely the lives of millions of people both directly and indirectly. It has affected the psychology of the people. The recent terror attack in Mumbai, India horrified the world. Emotionally we are still fresh with the memories of 26/11 of Mumbai, which unfortunately came from neighboring country. In spite of the geopolitical position, India was peaceful except the Naga insurgency problem. Of late, India has been experiencing internal attacks launched by its homegrown militant groups, especially in Jammu and Kashmir and in the northeastern states. The northeastern states of India in recent years, have experienced a series of indiscriminate bombings causing mass-casualty, kidnappings, and extortions masterminded by militant groups who want to 'secede' from India or want 'self-autonomy' (for e.g. Assam, Nagaland, and Tripura). These groups have a support base in their states for their cause. However, the type of activities they are involved in most cases have turned them into 'terrorist outfits'. The groups are involved in acts of intimidation, bombing, kidnapping, and extortion, that come under the definition of 'terrorism'. One of such organization, which is demanding a separate independent state, is 'United Liberation Front of Asom' (ULFA). For last three decades, ULFA has been taking a violent path to achieve this goal in Assam. The ULFA came into existence along with the 'Assam Movement' in 1979 against foreign nationals. The army atrocities committed during the movement provoked the secessionists stand among the few, which created an armed group like ULFA. Many cadres who joined ULFA were active participants in the movement, who were tortured brutally during that period. From the beginning, ULFA was involved with 'individuals killing' whom they thought were enemies of Assam and *'dacoities'* (robbery). In the initial phase, ULFA got people's support due to their 'Robinhood Image' and 'Anti-foreigners' stand. However, over the years, ULFA has changed its color. They no longer hold the 'Robinhood Image' and they have even changed their stand on immigration issue of the state. In the recent years, ULFA has killed innocent civilians not even sparing the schoolchildren during the Independence Day celebration in Dhemaji.

The study tries to explore as what is still keeping the outfit alive and how the civil society in Assam is responding to the violence inflicted by ULFA. Secondly, the ULFA seemed to enjoy mass popular support in the initial years of its formation, with the people generally heeding to its diktats in terms of boycott calls and the like, whether out of fear, charismatic characteristics of the leaders or due to their 'Robinhood image'. Thirdly, the support level of the ULFA has declined over the years, in the face of an unprecedented surge in terrorist activities on its part, coupled by the fact that the outfit is now widely believed to be under the influence of external forces (cross border linkages of actors). Lastly, the ULFA is sustaining due to a wide range of plausible factors like:

(1) Easy availability of small arms;

(2) Interests of vested groups driven by stakes in the "business" of terrorism;

(3) Presence of too many unemployed youths in the State who become easy targets for the outfit's recruitment drives; and

(4) Ideological concerns among its sympathizers within the State itself, might account for the sustenance of the struggle.

The Separatist Movements of the Fringe

The northeast region is a land of ethnic, cultural, and linguistic divergence. It consists of 160 scheduled tribes, over 400 tribal sub-tribal groups, and a large number of non-tribal population.[3] The population of the seven northeast Indian states (excluding Sikkim) accounts for 8.06 percent of India's total land and 3.73 percent of the population. All the northeastern states categorized as 'special category states' whose developmental fund's 90 percent is grant and only 10 percent is loan. This region has the highest rates of unemployment in the country, with a rate close to 12 percent as against the national average of 7.7 percent. The per capita income of the states of the region is also well below the national average (Rs.12,407 against Rs.17,978).[4]

The borders of Bangladesh, Bhutan, China, and Myanmar surround the northeast. Besides Jammu & Kashmir, northeast is one of the beautiful and naturally rich regions in the country. Like Jammu & Kashmir, it is also under the grip of insurgency and ethnic conflict. Out of the eight states of the northeast India, four states i.e. Assam, Manipur, Nagaland, and Tripura are boiling with ethnic unrest and insurgency at present. There are as many as 109-armed rebel groups operating in the Northeast region. Manipur tops the list with forty groups out of which six are banned and nine of these groups are active and twenty-five are inactive. Second is Assam with thirty-four rebel groups, two of which are banned with six active and twenty-six inactive armed groups. Meghalaya has four rebel groups out of which three are active and one inactive.

Mizoram has two rebel groups and both are listed as active. Nagaland has two active and two inactive groups. Tripura has two groups, which are banned in addition to one active and twenty-two inactive groups. Only Arunachal Pradesh so far has no rebel group yet.[5] Once Mizoram was also under a grip of secessionist movement but government of India oppressed it with a very firm hand. Of all the regions in the Indian sub-continent, the Northeastern frontier has been its most challenging sector. Inhabited by people of Southeast Asian origin, India's Northeast which is commonly referred to by a mono-syllable Northeast and its people as North-easterners has really no social or cultural affinity with the rest of the Indian polity, which is of Dravidian or Aryan descent.[6] The Khasis and Jaintias had a moderately developed economy as they were engaged with trade in the plains of Assam and Bangladesh. Manipur also underwent the process of state formation from relatively early times. Politically, all the states of northeast were different from each other. Except the separatist movements, these northeastern states are culturally, socially, politically and economically can not be put together in one pigeonhole. Northeasterners continue to face tremendous strife and emotional alienation from the rest of the country intensified by its geographical isolation.

The Naga insurgency, began as early as in 1950s has continued with varying degrees of intensity. The Naga insurgency later on played an important role in other secessionist movements in the region. The main reason of the Naga movement has been to have a 'Greater Nagaland' as a sovereign state comprising of all the Naga inhibited areas that covers parts of other states and parts of Myanmar. After the Government of India Act, 1935, when Burma was separated from India as another country, the Nagas made their first demand in 1937 before the Governor General of India. After Independence, the Nagas became tougher in their demands and launched a violent underground movement in early 1950s. The legendary Angami Zapu

Phizo went on to create a parallel government and a 'Naga Federal Army'. Various violent acts of sabotage and disruption in Nagaland forced the central government to call it an insurgency. The deployment of Indian Army and atrocities outraged the Naga people and brought them more closely to the underground government of Phizo. Though violent activities were abated when the state of Nagaland was formed in 1962 as a follow-up to the agreement with the Naga People's Convention, the violent outcomes continued with the passage of time. Then in 1980 under the leadership of Thuengaling Muivah, Isak Chisi Swu and S.S. Khaplang a new underground organization called the National Socialist Council of Nagaland (NSCN) was formed. This organization emerged as the most radical and powerful insurgent group fighting for the Naga cause, who later on helped many other underground organizations like ULFA and NDFB of Assam. However, in 1998 the NSCN split into two factions i.e. NSCN-IM (Isak-Muivah) and NSCN-K (Khaplang). At present both the group are in a ceasefire with the Government of India. In spite of several negotiations and ceasefire deals drawn on with Narasimha Rao, Deve Gowda and Vajpayee governments of the country, the insurgency is still on. The present government also continues the process of negotiation with NSCN, the last one that was held in January 2007. However, senior leader, R.H. Raising, has repeatedly said that they are not willing to give up their demand for a 'special federal relationship between India and Nagaland', which includes a separate Naga constitution and joint patrolling of international borders by India and Naga security forces.[7]

Insurgency in Mizoram developed from a sense of loss of identity to the 'Assamese Chauvinism'. This was one of the major factors that worked to the dissatisfaction of the Mizos. Mizoram was previously in the Hill District Council of Assam. The Mizo District Council asked the governor of Assam to take precautionary measures for the dreaded famine, which the Mizos predicted based on the Mizo calendar and cycle, following the flowering of bamboos. The Assam Government rejected the request, dismissing the prediction of the famine as a tradition of the 'primitive people'. However, the prediction proved right leading to slow supply of relief to the Mizo people. The Riang and Chakmas were eating wild *'arami'*, a kind of wild grass and there were reports of starvation deaths and plights of people from the famine-hit areas before the relief arrived.[8] The alleged neglect of the Mizos during the Great Famine in 1959-60 by the Assam and Union government led the Mizo National Front (MNF) to launch an insurgency movement with Pu Laldenga as its Chairman. The MNF right from the beginning made its military and secessionist intentions clear to the Mizo people, specially the youth. It propagated that before the coming of the British, the Mizos were an independent nation. The MNF also brought the religion factor; it portrayed India as a land of Hindus with Mizoram consisting of Christians.[9] The insurgency was dealt with lot of energy and with measures like grouping of villages, army operations, and curfew. The movement stopped with series of peace talks, negotiations, and settlement and finally signing of Mizo Accord on 20 June 1986. The insurgents and MNF leaders were absorbed in the national mainstream and it became a part of active political process of the state.

The armed conflict of Manipur is more complex and has historical roots to it. In the year 1948 under the leadership of Hijam Irabot Singh, a revolutionary movement was launched to liberate Manipur from the feudalism but this could not sustain due to his death in 1951. Manipur got its statehood in the year 1972, which led to disillusionment among the Meiteis (dominant community of Manipur besides the Nagas and Kukis). This gave a section of Meiteis a rise of political consciousness and quest for secessionism. Finally, in the year 1964 before getting the statehood Arambam Samarendra Singh founded the United National Liberation Front (UNLF) to achieve independence and establish a socialist country. In 1968, another breakaway group from

UNLF called the Revolutionary Government of Manipur (RGM) was formed under the leadership Oinam Sudhir Kumar. During Bangladesh liberation war, most of the secessionist leaders were arrested. Again, in 1978 N. Bisheswar formed another militant organization called the People's Liberation Army (PLA).[10] The population of Manipur can be grouped into two main ethnic communities: the Meiteis, who inhabit the valley and the twenty- nine tribes in the hills who can be divided into two main ethno-denominations namely Nagas and Kuki-Chins. The Meiteis are not only barred from the special constitutional privileges granted to Scheduled Tribes but also not allowed to settle in hill districts under the State Land Reform Act. There are no such restrictions for Nagas and Kukis who are Christians. This is one of the main tensions between the Meiteis and hill tribes. Therefore, the insurgency in Manipur has also divided into Meitei, Naga and Kuki groups. While the Meitei insurgents' prime objective is to free their pre-British territory from Indian occupation, the Naga insurgents of Manipur support the demand for a sovereign 'Nagalim (Greater Nagaland)'. The Kukis on the other hand supported the demand of a separate 'Kukiland' for which the Kukis in Burma is also fighting for. These insurresectionary groups have the ability to fight against the state for decades, as there is no dearth of extortion money, cross border linkages with like-minded groups and inflow of unemployed youth joining the outfits.[11] The insurgency problem in Manipur is still on and it is thriving more with extortion, cross border trade of small arms and drugs.

Tripura is the smallest landlocked states of seven states of northeast India. It was a princely state taken over by the Government of India on 15 October 1949. The insurgency problem in Tripura cropped up when there was a huge influx of Bengali population from the East Pakistan. The tribals in Tripura now account for forty-one percent of agricultural landless laborers and rest are non-tribals. The tribal population of Tripura consists of different ethnic groups, languages, and culture. The largest tribal groups are the 'Kokborok' language speaking tribes of the Tripuri, the Jamatia, the Reang and the Noatia tribal communities. However, Bengali is the accepted language of the state and has become the bone of contention between the tribals and non-tribals.[12] The tribal militant groups like the Sengkrak, the Tripura National Volunteers (TNV), the All-Tripura Tribal Force (ATTF), and the National Liberation Front of Tripura (NLTF) are some of the prominent groups operating there.[13] The ATTF is the most prominent group having established links with NSCN and ULFA. The reason behind the insurgency problem in this state is demographics, and this is the only state in India's northeast that has been transformed, in recent history, from a predominantly tribal to a predominantly non-tribal state. Tribal terrorist groups specifically target the non-tribal population, whom they call 'settler refugees'. Insurgent violence in the State dates back to the first Communist Party of India (CPI) led movement in 1948-51, but assumed its current contours of tribal vs. non-tribal violence through a succession of militant organizations and movements since the creation of the now defunct Tripur Sena in the early 1970s.[14] Despite its 74 percent literacy rate, the state ranks 22nd in the Human Resource Development Index and 24th in the Poverty Index of India in 1999.

The Naga Movement for an independent state, the Mizo rebellion, the indigenous insurgency in Tripura, the anti-foreigners movement in Assam and the search for a greater autonomy by Bodo inhabited areas in Assam are not in majority have been fuelled by the same core issue i.e. the strong desire of small but distinct communities, which have different ways of life and have managed their affairs in their own ways for long to preserve their cultural identities and their perceptions that these are under great threat.[15]

Origins of Insurgency in Assam

Assam is one of the diverse states of a diverse country where Aryans, Dravidians, Mongoloid, and other ethnic groups have created a distinct multicultural society. Before the British arrived in Assam, it was ruled by the Ahom kingdom. The mighty Ahoms ruled Assam for six hundred years. Assam was never a part of any empires of kings who ruled India but it shared a cultural interaction since the time of ancient Indian civilization.[16]

The socio-political history of Assam over the past three decades presents a gory and lingering phase of insurrection-propelled discord. The ball was set rolling by the formation of the United Liberation Front of Asom (ULFA) and memories of Assam Movement coupled with army atrocities and feeling of alienation in 1979. The emergence of the ULFA as a political force in the socio-political milieu of Assam and the space enjoyed by it, was, if anything, a reflection of the disillusionment of the people with the prevailing political environment coupled with a long held view among the people in general that Assam had always received a 'step motherly' treatment from the Union Government. Raising as it did the structural issue of internal colonization of Assam by New Delhi, ULFA maintained that this 'Colonial Rule of India' (over Assam) rested on extracting raw materials, resources and revenues from vast rural hinterlands of Assam and then finding out an easy market for the finished products elsewhere. The ULFA therefore demanded a '*Swadhin Asom*' (Independent/Sovereign Assam). However, over the years, the dynamics of the situation has been such that what started as an insurgent-separatist movement with the formation of the ULFA for securing a sovereign and independent Assam is increasingly degenerating into a theatre of bloodshed involving indiscriminate and mounting terrorist strikes in public places in different parts of Assam, claiming scores of innocent lives in the process. The situation is further aggravated by the presence of other sub-regional organizations operating within the State such as the Dima

Halam/Halim Daogah (DHD) in North Cachar Hills, The United Peoples' Democratic Solidarity (UPDS) in Karbi Anglong and The National Democratic Front of Bodoland (NDFB) in the Bodo inhabited areas, among others, each with its own agenda of political bargaining based on the use of violence. These low-intensity conflicts have attracted state intervention in a way that has, more often than not only gone to boost further violence than curbing it. In fact, the protracted low-intensity conflict as evident from the functioning of the ULFA and the state response to the same has seen Assam bleeding for almost three decades now. One expected fallout of the entire process has been that, in all of this it is the common people, who find themselves at the receiving end, caught as they are in the crossfire. Consequently, it is the ordinary citizen, who invariably has to endure the most of gross human rights violations from either side, be it mindless killings of innocent workers and bombings in public places by militants or security forces targeting helpless villagers on suspicion of being ULFA cadres while adopting a conventional military strategy based on a security dilemma. The outfit had lost 10,000 cadres and 30,000 of its cadres wounded.[17]

Methodology

The present study is a qualitative study where in depth interviews were conducted. For the interview purpose, a structured open-ended questionnaire was developed. The interviews took place with the researcher writing down or tape recorder was used to collect views of the civil society. Each interview lasted for about 45 to 60 minutes. To keep the views of the civil society as genuine as possible narratives method was used and at times their words and language were kept the same for the purpose. There were a total of fifty-four narratives in the study. The narratives were based on the dates of the fieldwork carried out during the study and location.

Field visits were undertaken in Tinsukia (Kakopathar, Tinsukia town, Jerai), Dibrugarh (Chabua, Nokhongia Gaon and Tengakhat), Nalbari (Ghograpara, Kotkia and Nalbari town) and Guwahati city. The civil society respondents were selected randomly based on their willingness to be interviewed. The interviews were carried out with regard to the following categories:

Representatives, from the civil society including senior citizens, youth representing organizations/political parties like All Assam Student's Union, Asom Jatiyotabadi Yuva Chatra Parishad, Asom Gana Parishad, Congress (I), women, teachers, social activists, writers, scholars and local media personnel from the state.

Study Area

The proposed study was carried out in the districts of Kamrup (Guwahati city), Tinsukia (Tinsukia town, Jerai and Kakopathar), Dibrugarh (Chabua, Nokhongia Gaon, and Tengakhat), and Nalbari district (Nalbari town and Ghograpara). These particular districts were selected keeping in mind the concentration of ULFA cadres and support base. Tinsukia, Dibrugarh and Nalbari districts have a history of a large number of cadres joining the outfit. During ULFA's heyday, there was a competition among the districts to send as many cadres as they could. The villagers even gave them a hero's welcome and farewell while joining the outfit.[18] However, according to the state police none of the districts is free of ULFA cadres. Guwahati city on the other hand is the gateway to Assam and other northeastern states. It also serves as a hiding place and is a victim of ULFA's terror strikes.

Tinsukia district of Assam has a unique history that sets it apart from the rest of others. The people of this area take pride in their history in terms of their kingdom and revolt against the mighty Ahoms who ruled Assam. The people of this district still take pride in it and think that outsiders are still exploiting them from their dues. Tinsukia district was known as Bangmara and Changmai Pathar before the British came in. It was the capital of Mottock Kingdom. The Mottock Kingdom occupied a distinct place in the history of Assam during the later part of the 18th century and the early part of 19th century. The Moamareeyas or the Mottoks turned the history of the mighty Ahom Kingdom by leading the historic Moamareeya Rebellion, which was the first socio-political movement in the history of Assam. Tinsukia District is situated in upper Assam and bounded by Arunachal Pradesh in the east. In the southwest by Dibrugarh district and in north by Dhemaji district which is separated from Tinsukia district by the mighty river Brahmaputra. In 1823, British first discovered tea plant in Sadiya and the first tea plantation was started in Chabua near Tinsukia. The name Chabua comes from word "Chah-Buwa"(Tea Plantation). In 1876, coal was found near Ledo and Margherita. In 1882 Crude Oil was discovered in Digboi and Country's first Oil well was built at Digboi in 1889 and the refinery, which was later built at Digboi was the first refinery in Asia and third in the world. In 1882, the Dibru-Sadiya Railway line was inaugurated through Tinsukia, which was the turning point in the political economy of northeast India.

Like Tinsukia, Dibrugarh district is also situated in the upper Assam. It is bounded by Dhemaji district on the north, Tinsukia district on the east, Tirap district of Arunachal district on the southeast, and Sibsagar district on the north and southwest. Dibrugarh district is flat with gradual slope from the east Arunachal hills to the west. Dibrugarh town is the district headquarter, situated on the southern bank of the Brahamaputra, it is connected by broad gauge railway line of Northeast Frontier Railway to the rest of the state and the country through Tinsukia. The National Highway 37 is the major road running through the district. Mohanbari airport is located at a distance of about sixteen Km from Dibrugarh town, which serves the upper Assam district of Dibrugarh, Tinsukia and Sivasagar and Arunachal Pradesh and is linked with Guwahati, Kolkata, and Delhi. Oil and tea are the major industries of the district. The Oil India

Ltd. headquarter is located at Duliajan, at a distance of about fifty kms from Dibrugarh town. The Fertiliser Corporation of India and Assam Petro-Chemicals Ltd. at Namrup and the Assam Gas Co. at Duliajan, NEEPCO near Duliajan are some of the other major industries in the district. Dibrugarh district is also very rich in terms of oil and tea and people here are proud of their resources. However, the feeling of exploitation and alienation is also strong among them.

Whereas, Nalbari and Kamrup districts are not rich in any natural resources like Dibrugarh and Tinsukia, the people of these two districts are mostly dependent on agriculture and there is no industrialization. Socio-economically these two districts are poor and backward compared to Tinsukia and Dibrugarh.

Nalbari district is situated in between Kamrup and Barpeta district. For better administration, old Kamrup district was divided into three districts and Nalbari is one of the districts. The northern side of the district is bounded by the Indo-Bhutan International boundary and the southern side by the mighty Brahmaputra. The Darrang and the Kamrup district fall in the east and the Barpeta district in the west. The district with nearly three per cent area of the state shelters about four per cent of the state's total population as per 2001 census. The density per sq. km. in the district is about five hundred persons as against three hundred and forty persons per square kilometer for the whole state. Nearly ninety-eight per cent of the total populations of the district live in villages and the economy of the district is based on agriculture.

Kamrup district comprises of two sub-divisions namely, Guwahati and Rangia and there are eight revenue circles under Guwahati sub-division and three revenue circles under Rangia sub-division. Furthermore, the district is divided into fifteen development blocks. The district is surrounded by Udalguri and Baska district on the north and Meghalaya on the south. Darrang district and Kamrup metropolitan district surrounds Kamrup on the east and Goalpara district and Nalbari district are situated at the west. The capital city Guwahati is under Kamrup metropolitan district. Majority of the population in the district is rural (about sixty-five per cent) though it is lower than other districts and density of population is about six hundred persons per square kilometer.

REFERENCES

1. Referred in Chakravorti, Ravi, 1994, *Terrorism: Past, Present and Future*, www.jstor.org, p. 2340

2. Crenshaw, Martha, 2000, *The Psychology of Terrorism: An Agenda for the 21st Century*, www.jstor.org, p.406

3. Das, Samir Kumar, 2007, *Conflict and Peace in India's Northeast: The Role of Civil Society*, Policy Studies 42, East- West Center, Washington, p. 75

4. Pandey, Nishchal N, 2008, *India's North-Eastern Region: Insurgency, Economic Development and Linkages with South-East Asia*, Manohar Publishers & Distributors, New Delhi, pp. 13, 14, 15

5. Baruah, Sanjib,2007, *Postfrontier Blues: Toward a New Policy Framework for Northeast India*, Policy Studies 33, East-West Center Washington, p. 9

6. Mukhim, Patricia, Where is this North-east, in Geeti Sen (ed.), 2006, *Where The Sun Rises When Shadows Fall The North-east*, Oxford University Press, New Delhi, p.177

7. Pandey, pp. 30, 31

8. Nag, Sajal, 2002, *Contesting Marginality: Ethnicity, Insurgency and Subnationalism in North-East India,* Manohar Publishers & Distributors, New Delhi, pp. 217, 218

9. *Ibid.*, 20, 21.

10. Kh, Devi, Elizabeth, 2006, *A Study on the Social Background of Insurgents in Assam with Special Reference to ULFA*, Peace Studies, OKDISCD, Guwahati, (Unpublished Research Study), pp. 24,25

11. Pandey, pp. 34, 35, 36
12. *Ibid.*, 37.
13. Bhaumik, Subir, 'Taming the Twipra Tempest' in Jaideep Saikia (ed.), 2007, *Frontier in Flames: Northeast India in Turmoil*, Penguin Books India Ltd., New Delhi, pp. 101, 102
14. Sahni Ajai, *Tripura: The Politics of Ethnic Terror*, www.satp.org, accessed on 20.01.2009
15. Sinha, K.K, 'Insurgency in the North-East: An Overview,' in Dipankar Sengupta, Sudhir Kr. Singh (ed.), 2004, *Insurgency in North-East India: The Role of Bangladesh*, AuthorsPress, New Delhi, p. 30
16. Gogoi, Dilip, 'Quest for Swadhin Asom: Explaining Insurgency and the Role of the State in Assam' in Dipankar Sengupta, Sudhir Kumar Singh (ed.), 2004, *Insurgency in North-East India: The Role of Bangladesh*, Authorpress Global Network, New Delhi, p. 40
17. Goswami, Mamoni Raisom, 'Peace Talk: A Prelude' in Anuradha Dutta, Ratna Bhuyan (ed.), 2007, *Genesis of Conflict and Peace*, Akansha Publishing House, New Delhi, p.7
18. One of the surrendered ULFA members shared this information with the researcher.

2

Backdrop

I

The 'seven sisters' that is how describes northeast India, is going through a phase where out of the seven states, four states are reeling with conflict. Assam is the recent one to enter into an armed conflict; however, it is in the third decade of the secessionist demand from India. The demand for a '*Swadhin Asom*' (Independent Assam) by United Liberation Front of Asom (ULFA) has taken an ugly turn in the state in terms of development and safety of the people and the region. In 1979 Assam under the leadership of All Assam Students Union (AASU) launched a massive agitation against the unlawful influx of the foreigners from neighboring country Bangladesh. Number of organizations supported the movement; in fact, Ms. Indu Prabha Baruah (Assam Pradeshik Mahila Samiti) said, "the boys are doing an excellent work". This agitation continued for another six years. Along with the Assam Movement, simultaneously another group of boys emerged during the same period, which led to a growth of an extremists group later on. This group of boys gathered on the ground of *Rang Ghar*, the ancient amphitheater of the Ahom Kingdom situated in Sibsagar District of upper Assam. This was the beginning of a new phase in the history of Assam.

The group of boys who were present at the meeting of *Rang Ghar* was Rajib Rajkonwar, Paban Baruah, Golap Barua and Samiran Gogoi. All of them assumed different names later on and in fact, they were more famous with their pseudonyms. Thus, Rajib Rajkonwar we know as Arabinda Rajkhowa, the Chairman of ULFA Golap Barua as Anup Chetia, the outfit's general secretary, and Samiran Gogoi is actually Pradip Gogoi, the Vice-chairman of ULFA and Paban Baruah became Paresh Baruah. If we analyze the composition of the group, we can see people belonging to different age groups. Although younger to the other three, Paresh Baruah became the commander-in-chief, the military supreme of the outfit. ULFA also had different prominent mentors like Bhim Kanta Borgohain, an elderly Ahom of Sikhowaghat[1] and Bhadreshwar Gohain (first Chairman of the outfit) who went to serve as the Deputy Speaker of the State Legislative Assembly after elected on an AGP ticket.[2] This indicates the relationship shared by ULFA and AGP in the later years to come. All the members except Paresh Baruah were members of Asom Jatiyotabadi Yuva Chatra Parishad (AJYCP), a group that works with the youth of Assam besides AASU. This group of boys, aware of AASU's plan to launch an anti-foreigner's movement, felt that an armed battle would make Delhi to take notice of the whole situation here in Assam. However, these boys remained passive for another six years[3].

At some point in 1983, a group of boys in Tezpur formed an organization called Assam People Liberation Army (APLA). It had identical aims with ULFA and was better organized and well spread in the lower Assam areas. By 1985, APLA members merged with ULFA, which strengthened the organization a lot in the coming years.

It was not before late 1983 and early 1984 that large-scale recruitment in the ULFA began. The early inductions came from all across the state but one district, Nalbari, provided perhaps the highest number of cadres. Nalbari is barely one hundred Km west of Guwahati and it is bordering Bhutan. Nalbari was one of the fertile grounds for ULFA as this district was one of the poorest in comparison to the others with a better level of literacy rate (fifty six per cent).

This district remains flooded for three to four months every year loosing its crops where ninety per cent of the population is dependent on it. Many prominent leaders of ULFA like Sashadhar Choudhury, Raju Baruah and Pranati Deka have emerged from this district. Two kinds of boys and girls joined the outfit, one group consisted of simple villagers, who went for training and came back toughened and to some extent dedicated. Some of them were highly dedicated and motivated and in encounters later with the Army and Para Military Forces preferred to die rather than being captured. The second group consisted of mainly urban boys who were dropouts from school and were indulging in petty crime. This group was to be the nemesis of ULFA, later on.[4] Getting adequate recruits was not a problem for the outfit as poverty, unemployment supported it, and another bonus for them was the election of 1985 when Asom Gana Parishad (AGP) came into power of the state. The boys had an easy access in the corridors of power during AGP's period as many of the young leaders were close to the outfit that was not banned at that time. From 1988 to 1990, ULFA's violent activities escalated. It virtually controlled the state, extorting large sums from tea planters group and other businesspersons to finance its efforts, engaging in kidnappings and assassinating key political officials and police officers. Evidence of these abuses became known when a mass grave containing more than eleven bodies were uncovered at Lakhipathar, the headquarters of the commander-in-chief of the ULFA. The ruling AGP appeared to vacillate in its policy on ULFA, taking police action against suspected members of the group while appearing to maintain close ties to its leadership.

II

In the ULFA movement, it is believed that it received external help. According to the Government of India, it possesses 'impeccable evidence', which can prove the involvement of the neighboring countries.[5] One of the important cadres of APLA that merged with ULFA was Munim Nobis, who was later on to establish ULFA's ties with Pakistan's Inter Services

Intelligence (ISI). He also led the first 'external mission' of ULFA to Bangladesh and set up its 'foreign office' there.[6] Anup Chetia, Arabinda Rajkhowa and Pradip Gogoi went and established contact with the National Socialist Council of Nagaland (NSCN), one of the most powerful insurgent organizations in the northeast. Later on Paresh Baruah negotiated with the Kachin Independence Army (KIA) while visiting the NSCN headquarters for the training of the cadres in Myanmar.[7]

The ULFA sought shelter in the forests on the Indo-Bhutan border from the early 1990s and established several camps in the forest areas of southern Bhutan. The ULFA's Bhutan set-up had a reported strength of around two thousand cadres spread across the outfit's 'General Head Quarters', it's 'Council Head Quarters', a 'Security-cum-Training Camp' and a well-concealed 'Enigma Base'. Most camps and other establishments of the ULFA were in Sandrup Jongkhar, a district in southern Bhutan that borders Assam's Nalbari district. However, during the military operations launched in December 2003 all the outfit's camps and observation posts were destroyed. ULFA also established links with the Afghan Mujahideen. Reports indicate that at least two hundred ULFA activists received training in Pakistan and Afghanistan. Seized documents and interrogation of some arrested cadres of ULFA revealed that the Defense Forces Intelligence (DFI) of Bangladesh had also trained them in the Sylhet district and several camps were there in Bangladesh. The ISI and the Directorate General of Field Intelligence (DGFI) of Bangladesh were agencies that reportedly have been facilitating the ULFA's presence and operations. Several details of ULFA's Bangladesh connection were exposed when the Bangladeshi authorities arrested one of the prominent leaders Anup Chetia on December 21, 1997. He is currently under detention at the high-security Dhaka Central Jail. The main charges against Chetia include illegal entry into Bangladesh, possession of two forged Bangladeshi passports, possession of an unauthorized satellite telephone and illegal possession of foreign currency of countries as diverse as the

US, UK, Switzerland, Thailand, Philippines, Spain, Nepal, Bhutan, Belgium, Singapore and others. Two other accomplices, identified as Babul Sharma and Laxmi Prasad, were also arrested along with him. Apart from running training camps, ULFA launched several income generating projects in Bangladesh. It has set up a number of firms in Dhaka, including media consultancies and soft drink manufacturing units. Besides, it is reported to own three hotels, a private clinic, and two motor driving schools in Dhaka. It is reported that Paresh Baruah personally owns or has controlling interests in several businesses in Bangladesh, including a tannery, a chain of departmental stores, garment factories, travel agencies, shrimp trawlers, and transport and investment companies.[8]

According to recent Seventh Border Coordination Development Meeting on 4 August 2009, ULFA and NDFB militants, based in Assam, are regrouping and may try to enter Bhutan to set up camps. The Assam government had conveyed this information during the seventh border coordination development meeting between Bhutan and the Indian state of Assam last month. The Assam government also said that these insurgent groups are also in close collaboration with anti-national groups like the Communist Party of Bhutan, Bhutan Tiger Force (BTF) and Revolutionary Youth of Bhutan (RYOB). Intelligence reports from Assam says that the ULFA and Bodo militants had suffered a severe setback after operation flush out in 2003, after which they took shelter in neighboring countries like Bangladesh and Myanmar. However, according to Indian media, with an India friendly government in Bangladesh and growing ties between India and Myanmar, recently the groups are under pressure to leave these areas.[9]

III

The Union Government's response to the uprisings in the northeast has been two-branched strategy of tough counter-insurgency combined with development aid to end the popular grievances. In Assam, to repress ULFA, the Government of

India declared ULFA unlawful on 27 November 1990, and on 29 November, the first army operation was launched under the name of 'Operation Bajrang'. Most of the forty hideouts of ULFA were deserted and weapons were taken away. This followed by election in the state and Hiteswar Saikia becoming the Chief Minister of Assam. After coming to power he released four hundred fifty out of six hundred sixty suspected militants arrested during Operation Bajrang to initiate 'peace processes'[10]. Unfortunately, the peace process could not sustain long as this followed by 'Operation Rhino', which was preceded by 'Operation Cloudburst' that started in the first week of September 1991 to crush the dens of ULFA along the Arunachal-Nagaland border of Assam. Operation Rhino continued as part II with renewed gusto on 9 January 2007 again.[11] Besides this, the Hiteswar Saikia regime also offered the ULFA cadres to surrender and get incentives to start a better peaceful life! These incentives brought back many of 'our deviant boys' to the mainstream, who later on played an important role in Prafulla Kumar Mahanta's tenure as the next Chief Minister. According to Justice (Retd.), K.N Saikia Commission of Inquiry on 'Secret Killings' carried out between the year 1998 and 2001, after studying thirty five cases of the nature of secret killing in four phases, in its report held Praffula Kumar Mahanta the then Chief Minister as well as in charge of the Home Department responsible for the cases. The panel also indicted independent legislator Kushal Deori in one case of mass murder that was the murder of suspected ULFA conduit Uma Gogoi's family. In his report, Justice Saikia reported that the killings were the outcome of a nexus between the police and the surrendered ULFA members collectively referred as SULFA[12]. The Commission said that the firearms used by the killers were normally found with the police and military personnel, the Saikia Commission said police was patrolling the area prior and after the killings, but not when they took place.

Besides these measures, the government of India has also imposed the infamous Armed Forces (Special Powers)

Act (AFSPA) in Assam. The AFSPA was designed to combat the Naga rebellion. This act provides the legal framework for counterinsurgency operations against numerous armed rebellions in the northeast region. The act has been amended a number of times to accommodate changes in the names and number of states. It now applies to all of Northeast India. This controversial act includes the power of the security forces to make preventive arrests, search premises without warrant, and shoot and kill civilians and effective legal immunity of soldiers implicated in such actions, since court proceedings are contingent on the central government's prior approval (Government of India 1958).[13] It is important to note that the Justice B. P. Jeeven Reddy Commission, deputed to study and report to the government of India about the AFSPA has recommended to the government of India an immediate withdrawal of the law from Manipur. The Commission filed its report to the government in 2005. The Prime Minister of India responded by stating in a press conference that the law will be withdrawn as early as possible. Since then nothing is heard about the government's plan to do so. In fact, it will be nearly six years that Irom Chanu Sharmila has been on her hunger strike demanding AFSPA's withdrawal from her state.

In January 2007, the ULFA, faced with the pressures of an intense counterinsurgency operation in the rural areas of Upper Assam, as it targeted Hindi-speaking communities of the same area for attack. The victimized ethnic communities called for the army to provide protection. The government in response launched a tougher counterinsurgency operation. For India, the display and use of military power has become a routine way of asserting state sovereignty in the northeast. Interestingly, in 2005 and 2006 when there was widespread popular support for negotiations between the government and the ULFA in Assam, senior figures in India's counterinsurgency establishment, notably the Governor of Assam, Lieutenant General Ajai Singh, publicly opposed negotiations on grounds that a military victory against ULFA was within reach.[14]

According to India Human Rights Report 2007 in the name of counterinsurgency, the police continued to use firearms indiscriminately against civilians. Many civilians fell to police bullets while exercising their fundamental right to protest against injustice and illegal activities of the security forces. The incidents of killing in police firing included killing of at least eight civilians at Kakopathar and Makum in Tinsukia district on 10 February 2006. Another killing incident of a youth at Panigaon in North Lakhimpur on 22 March 2006. Then killing of three persons including two school children at Moirabari in Morigaon district on 18 November 2006, and killing of Tabibor Rahman in police firing at Rangiya in Kamrup district on the night of 4 October 2006.[15] All these incidences proved the attitude of the government when it came to repressing turmoil in northeast India.

Apart from military means, counter-insurgency has included a variety of crude political methods. For instance, members of rebel groups are offered financial incentives to surrender- often leading to splits within the insurgent groups, with an opportunity for state intelligence outfits to recruit members of surrendered factions for counterinsurgency operations in return for security against their former comrades. This is what exactly happened with ULFA.

Carrot and stick approach has been the preferred way of the government of India to deal with insurgency in the Northeast. Under this approach, the government has been increasing the pressure of law enforcement agencies on the insurgent outfits so that they can be brought to the negotiating table. ULFA has been engaged in peace talks with the Centre since September 2005. This was the time when ULFA-nominated Peoples' Consultative Group (PCG) started talks with the government. The government unilaterally declared ceasefire on August 13, 2006 but was forced to call it off on September 24, 2006 as ULFA continued with its violent activities. The government was willing to accept some of the demands of ULFA but wanted the outfit to commit itself to the talks. ULFA was not ready for this. It appears ULFA was only interested in getting its five jailed leaders freed, and using the peace talks as a ploy. The state government of Assam, which has been advocating a negotiated solution with ULFA in recent times, has now realized its mistake. Speaking to media in Guwahati on January 15 Assam Chief Minister, Tarun Gogoi admitted that his government's six-week ceasefire with the outlawed ULFA was a mistake because it helped the rebels to take advantage to regroup and spread out their cadres across the state. He reportedly said, "In retrospect, I admit the judgment may be a little wrong when we offered a ceasefire to ULFA...our intentions were positive and in good faith thinking that ULFA would come for peace talks. But they utilized the truce to regroup, collect arms and then spread out their cadres to different parts of the state." Recently, Chief Minister in his Independence Day speech said that Assam would have a scheme for the rehabilitation of the militants who give up arms and return to the mainstream. He appealed to all militant outfits to give up arms and come to the negotiating table if they wanted Assam's development. At the same time, Gogoi warned that the state government would come down heavily on violence by extremists and was determined to curb their activities[16].

So far, the government of India has adopted that the unrest in the region has to be dealt as a law and order issue. The core issues and demands are not taken into account from the beginning to the end.

REFERENCES

1. Rammohan, E.N, 2005, *Insurgent Frontiers: Essays from the Northeast*, India Research Press, New Delhi, p.40

2. Routray, Bibhu Prashad, 16.07.08, *ULFA: The Revolution Comes Full Circle*, www.satp.org/publication/faultline/volume13/article6.htm, p. 1.

3. Gokhale, Nitin , 1998, *The Hot Brew: The Assam Tea Industry's Most Turbulent Decade (1987-1997)*, Spectrum Publications, Guwahati, pp. 16, 17.

4. Rammohan, pp. 45, 46.
5. Das, Samir Kumar, 1994, *ULFA: A Political Analysis*, Ajanta Publications, New Delhi, p. 45.
6. Mahanta, Nani, 2005, *Terrorism in Assam: The Case of ULFA*, Unpublished Doctoral Thesis, Department of Political Science, Gauhati University, Guwahati, p. 115
7. Gokhale, pp. 17, 18 & 21.
8. United Liberation Front of Asom (ULFA)- Terrorists Group of Assam, 11.08.09, www.satp.org
9. Lamsang, Tenzing, *Militants Regrouping to enter Bhutan: Assam Government (Reproduction)*, www.apfanews.com, 04.08.09
10. Das, p. 85
11. Das, Samir Kumar, 'Peace sans Democracy: A Study of Ethnic Peace Accords in Northeast India' in Sanjib Baruah (ed.), 2009, *Beyond Counter Insurgency: Breaking the Impasse in Northeast India*, Oxford University Press, New Delhi, p.247
12. Goswami Pandey, Rituparna, *Secrete Killing Still a Secrete*, , www.assamtimes.org, 15.11.07
13. Baruah, Sanjib,2007, *Postfrontier Blues: Toward a New Policy Framework for Northeast India*, Policy Studies 33, East- West Center Washington, p. 2
14. *Ibid.*, p. 10, 15
15. Asian Center for Human Rights, www.achrweb.org., 17.08.09
16. Sushanta Talukdar,www.thehindu.com, 16.08.2009

3

Feeling of Alienation

I

The ULFA movement has continued to sustain over the years. The question that arises here is what keeps it still alive. It is alleged that in the last decade or so, the organization has forged a nexus with countries and forces, which are profoundly inimical to the interests of Assamese society. However, it makes sense that external support alone could not possibly be the only source of its strength. Is it then that the ULFA has been able to build a strong network of shelter and support in some pockets of the state?

In this context, the role of the civil society in Assam needs to be critically examined in the background of the overall dynamics of political violence in terms of its stance on specific issues, which in turn would be shaped by its own internal vibrancy and mutual dialogue and networking taking place among its various components. A cursory glance at the role of the civil society vis-à-vis the insurgency situation in Assam over the years would indicate that its reaction to the whole issue has been subdued and fragmented. Accordingly, it is pertinent to analyze the civil society in Assam in a historical continuum vis-à-vis the entire gamut of the insurgency situation from the early years of its advent to the present.

Looking at northeast India, civil society groupings could be seen to be playing a significant role in the backdrop of a conflict-ridden scenario. For instance, in Nagaland, the Naga Hoho, a tribe based apex body of the Nagas, as well as the Naga Mothers Association (NMA) with its theme 'Shed No More Blood', are playing a prominent role in the peace movement. Similarly, the '*Meira Paibis* (women activist groups)' in Manipur have arguably achieved a certain level of mobilization vis-à-vis the peace initiative. In Assam, the '*Mahila Shanti Sena*' that is working under Tamulpur Anchalik Gramdan Sangh (TAGS) Kumarikata organization, has been working for peace and development in the region. The *Mahila Shanti Sena* members are women and they are believers of peace and non-violence. The activists from this group are involved with dispute settlement to caring for the sick as well as engaged in income generating constructive work.[1] At times organizations like *Matri Manch, Anchalik Mahila Sajagata Samiti* and *Chapar Anchalik Mahila Samiti* are some of the organizations, which played a significant role in mobilizing women against army atrocities during army operations in the state.[2] The AASU and AJYCP are also two prominent students' wing playing a very important role in socio-political milieu of the state.

The civil society in Assam while addressing the conflict situation appears to be vague in nature as opposed to operating through compact focused organizations based on strong social capital. Although of late there have been some sporadic incidents of public outcry against the vitiating atmosphere of violence in the state, it is imperative for the civil society in Assam to intervene more assertively in engaging with terrorism, based on a composite and multilateral dialogue process involving various segments of the civil society as an "initiative from below", given the persistence and sustenance of the ULFA led insurgency for so long a period.

The civil society in Assam got its representation through the middle class. The emergence of the Assam Association in 1903 gave a voice to Regional (Assamese) Nationalism. This Association was instrumental in voicing the grievances of Assamese middle class and it was instrumental in preparing the new generation in fighting against the British. Then the first students' organization *'Assam Chatra Sanmilan'* came into being in the year 1916. This followed by the establishment of *'Assam Sahitya Sabha'* in 1916 under the leadership of Lakhinath Bezbarua. The *'Assam Sahitya Sabha'* played an important role in Assamese nationalism in the years to come.[3]

During this time, the Assamese public opinion started to be increasingly agitated over the occupation of cultivable land by immigrants who came mainly from East Bengal. Immigrant leaders like Maulana Bhasani started demanding the abolition of the Line System, which was introduced in 1920 to protect the land rights of the indigenous peoples. Between 1930 to1936 as many as fifty nine grazing, forest, and village reserves were thrown open in Nowgong (now Nagaon) district under the colonization Scheme for settling the immigrants. It was against such a background the Assamese middle class intellectuals like Ambikagiri Raichoudhury and Jnananath Bora wrote about the need to defend the Assamese homeland against 'foreign' incursions. Raichoudhury was the first to put forward the idea of an Indian Federation of linguistic nationalities with dual citizenship.[4] Raichoudhury propagated the issues of Assam however, he was not a secessionist. He wanted that all regions of India should be able to preserve its own linguistic cultural heritage within India.[5]

When, after Independence, the Congress government in Assam failed to provide adequate checks to infiltration from newly created East Pakistan, Raichoudhury and his organization *'Asom Sangrakshini Sabha'* and *'Asom Jatiya Mahasabha'* started espousing the issues of illegal infiltration and land grabing, hegemony of Bengali language, census problem and issues concerning the indegeneous population etc.[6] However, Ambikagiri Raichoudhury remained a lonely voice in the first two decades or so of post-Independent Assam dominated by Congress politics veering sharply in favour of pan-Indian nationalism. The successful resistance put up against the grouping scheme by the Assam Congress under Gopinath Bordoloi's leadership and separation of Sylhet had greatly eased Assamese fears of losing their identity and from the fifties to the early sixties regional nationalist forces had to take a backseat. It was from the early seventies that Raichoudhury's ideas started finding favor with a section of the post-nineteen sixty generation of Assamese who had become increasingly aware of the colonial pattern of exploitation of Assam by the center as well as the growing threat posed by infiltration of foreigners into the state.[7]

The idea of a '*Swadhin Asom*' was shared by many other Assamese intellectuals of the pre-Independence period. Jnananath Bora, in his articles published in the Assamese journal *Awahon*, and in the newspaper, *Dainik Batori*, put forward his ideas of a sovereign Assam. Bora's idea's incorporated in his writings found expression during the Assam Movement (1979-85) on the foreigner's issue. These included the concept of economic independence, the need to bring the different tribal communities within the ambit of Assamese '*jatiatabad*', the development of the state's resources for the benefit of indigenous people and the idea of internal colonization. Bora may be, said to be one of those Assamese intellectuals who, in the nineteen thirties, tried to project the thesis that in order to avoid being colonially exploited by India, Assam must become independent and manage her own resources. Fifty years later, Jnananath Bora's views would find acceptance among a section of the Assamese youth who would resort to arms in order to liberate Assam from the 'Indian Colonial Yoke'. However, just as Jnananath Bora or Ambikagiri Raichoudhury did not have any clear perception about the position of the different nationalities within a '*Swadhin Asom*', the ULFA too has little to say about the nature of ethnic equations in a liberated homeland.

'*Prantik*' a pioneering and popular Assamese fortnightly magazine conducted a poll on 1 July, 1984 to gauge the people's mood towards the Assam Movement. The sample was of two thousand readers where it came out that about eighty two per cent thought that non-violent measures ought to be resorted to create pressure on the government. While, three per cent thought that negotiated settlement with the government was appropriate whereas another three per cent felt that violent protest was the only option left to the Assamese people.[8] According to another newspaper report, the civil society in Assam held meetings on issues like '*Ugrapanthi Sangathanar Kono Sadyasyak Ashraydan Diyar Birodhita Kara* (opposing shelter to any member of the militant outfit in the village)'. Moreover, the places where these meetings are organized were known to be areas sympathetic to the ULFA. The report says sixty villages under sixteen police stations in Sibsagar district have decided not to provide shelter to ULFA cadres and in lower Assam districts like Nalbari, Barpeta, and Kamrup people took out processions opposing the cult of violence and the militant outfit's activities.[9] In another incident of the civil society of lower Assam districts organized a meeting where '*Santras Birodhi Gana Manch* (Anti-terrorism People's Front)' organizers Umesh Rabha and Bipin Kalita asked for government's protection but later on Umesh Rabha was killed by the extremists after making several attempts in his life.[10]

ULFA also saw the most popular demonstrations against them from the civil society in the wake of the abduction and killing of Sanjay Ghosh in Majuli, the world's largest riverine island situated in Assam. When, two of Ghosh's alleged abductors were shot dead in Majuli, local residents of Kamalabari reportedly shouted slogans in support of the police action. That could have been beginning of what turned out to be rapid erosion of popular support for ULFA, which could not afford to remain oblivious to these happenings.[11] Another incident was the public outrage against bomb blasts by ULFA on August 15, 2004, at Dhemaji, upper Assam that killed a total of thirteen people, majority of women, and schoolchildren who had come to take part in the Independence Day celebration.

In the recent times however, the killing of an alleged ULFA cadre in Kakopathar in February 2006 showed another face of the civil society where they were not taking 'encounter deaths' by the paramilitary forces for granted. While protesting the killing of a suspected ULFA militant and another five villagers of Kakopathar, took a violent turn when the military opened fire at them as the public stoned a *jawan* to death.[12]

II

However, the 19th and 20th centuries have been marked by the rise of two increasingly powerful social entities: the nation and the market economy. Nevertheless, the society must never forget that these two entities depend on the fragile web of civil society, which is also the source of a great deal of the meaning of our existence and identity. The society is social beings before political or economic beings. Civil society consists of all the social groups and social relationships in which embedded are the families, communities, religious organizations, ethnic groups, schools, neighborhoods, sports teams, and voluntary associations, professional or occupational associations. These nodes of civil society are seedbeds for the social values, norms, and practices that are essential to the operation of both states and markets as well as to the general functioning of social life.[13]

Civil society refers to the arena of uncoerced collective action around shared interests, purposes, and values. It commonly embraces a diversity of spaces, actors, and institutional forms, varying in their degree of formality, autonomy, and power. Civil societies are often populated by organizations such as registered charities, non-governmental organizations, community groups, women's organizations, faith-based organizations, professional associations, trade unions, self-help groups, business associations, coalitions, and advocacy group. 'Associationalism' plays an important role in the whole concept of civil society.[14] The term civil society also refers to the quality of social life, including safety, mortality, civility, respect for diversity, and social order according to Persell.[15]

Traditionally, social scientists believed that the society lived in a two-sector world. There was the market or the economy on the one hand, and the state or government on the other. However, the general disenchantment with the overreach of the state in both the advanced capitalist and the developing world in the late 1980s and the early 1990s was to propel an important move—that of directing attention to the 'third sphere' in the form of the civil society in terms of a renewal of associational life invoking properties of social capital and trust at the community level. If the state is characterized by the logic of power as a means and an end, and the market is characterized by the logic of cold calculation based on profit and loss, the logic of civil society must necessarily be different to both the state and the economy, simply because it is expected to provide an antidote to both even as completely different sets of emotions and completely different sets of human interaction run the argument, define civil society, and demarcate it from the state and the economy.[16] The origins of the idea of civil society as a 'third sphere' lie in the formulations of Alexis de Tocqueville, who has been rediscovered along with civil society. He said that the monarchy and then the revolution in France had destroyed all intermediary associations between the individual and the state. Such a turn of events could culminate in a subtle despotism, argued Tocqueville, for citizens can fall prey to a tutelary power that dwarfs them. Spatially spread out intermediary associations could on the other hand, give to the citizens a taste of self-rule.[17] At another level the civil society refers to the amorphous intermediate space represented by institutions between the family and the state; a space which is free of both kinship relations and those determined by the state. In the context of the developing world, non-performance on the part of the state in terms of delivering the basic goods and services to its citizens have also significantly contributed to the resurgence of the notion of civil society as a panacea to a non-performing and now retreating state. Where the state fails to guarantee the autonomy of the individual, protection of the individual right to equal citizenship and access to the decision-making apparatus and participatory democratic framework and instead functions as an instrument subserving dominant sectional interests only, non-state associations and voluntary mobilizations would rise.[18] With specific reference to India, the analysis of the intermediate space constituted by civil society can hardly ignore the existence of primordial groups and traditional institutions. The image of civil society has had strong significance among reformers in India. Critics of the developmental state argue for decentralization to local communities or voluntary development groups to serve the need of the people better. Fundamental to each of these persuasions is belief in the significance of civil society to democratic governance.[19] Especially in Assam from the beginning of Assam Movement, the issues raised were related to the rights of the people over their resources and matters concerning good governance. The civil society in Assam demanded their basic rights through both peaceful as well as violent ways and ULFA is the reflection of the violent mood. However, at present it turned out to be a different scene altogether but ULFA had a support base in the civil society in the initial stage.

REFERENCES

1. Bhuyan, Abhijit, 2006,*Gandhian Non-Violence as a Means of Dispute Settlement in Assam: A Case Study of Tamulpur Anchalik Gramdan Sangh, Kumarikata,* Peace Studies, OKDISCD, Guwahati, pp. 55, 58

2. Goswami, Triveni, 2006, *Role of Women as Peace Builders with Special Reference to Nagaland*, Peace Studies, OKDISCD, Guwahati, p. 12

3. Mahanta, Nani, 2005, *Terrorism in Assam: The Case of ULFA*, Unpublished Doctoral Thesis, Department of Political Science, Gauhati University, Guwahati, p.36

4. Misra, Udayon, 2000, *The Periphery Strikes Back: Challenges to the Nation- State in Assam and Nagaland,* Indian Institute of Advanced Study, Shimla, pp. 84, 85

5. *Ambikagiri Raichoudhury Rachanawali*, 1986, Assam Prakashan Parishad, Guwahati,p. 13
6. *Ibid.*, p. 11.
7. Misra, pp. 86, 87.
8. Das, Samir Kumar, 1994, *ULFA: A Political Analysis*, Ajanta Publications, New Delhi, pp. 40, 41.
9. Patwary, Ajit, *"ULFA facing Alienation from the Masses"* referred in Nani Mahanta's Terrorism in Assam: The Case of ULFA, Doctoral Thesis (Unpublished), Department of Political Science, Gauhati University, Guwahati, p. 203.
10. *Ibid.* pp. 204, 205.
11. Das, Samir Kumar, 2007, *Conflict and Peace in India's Northeast: The Role of Civil Society*, Policy Studies 42, East- West Center, Washington, p. 50.

12 *Ibid.*, p. 51.

13 Persell, Caroline Hodges, 26/09/2008, Taking Society Seriously, www.jstor.org, pp. 641, 642.

14 Chandoke, Neera, 2003, *The Conceits of Civil Society*, Oxford University Press, New Delhi, p. 41.

15 Persell, Caroline Hodges, 26/09/2008, The Interdependence of Social Justice and Civil Society, www.jstor.org, p. 150.

16 Chandoke, Neera, 2003, *The Conceits of Civil Society*, Oxford University Press, New Delhi, p. 43

17 *Ibid* p. 42.

18 Dhanagare, D.N., 'Civil Society, State and Democracy: Contextualizing a Discourse' in N. Jayaram (ed.), 2005, *On Civil Society—Issues and Perspectives*, Sage Publications, New Delhi, p. 63.

19 Elliott, Carolyn M., 2003, *Civil Society and Democracy: A Reader*, Oxford University Press, New Delhi, p. 3.

4

Changing Popular Perception of Freedom

This chapter contains the narratives of the civil society respondents who voiced their views regarding the armed conflict in the state. The first parts of the narratives were carried out in Kakopathar, Jerai, and Tinsukia Town. The second part covers Chabua, Nokhongia Gaon, and Tengakhat of Dibrugarh district. The third part covers the civil society respondents of Ghograpara, Kotkia, and Nalbari town. The last part covers the Guwahati city of Kamrup district.

I

Ms. Khiroda Sonowal (48 years) is a primary school teacher. We had a pleasant chat before getting into the proper interview. Conversation with her showed that once she supported ULFA but not anymore. At present, she and her group of women are involved with many activities, which give a glimpse of hope in terms of civil society's role in a place like Kakopathar. The excerpts of the interview are as follows.

Presently Ms. Sonowal is the vice president of the local *Mahila Samiti* (Women's Organization) and a member of Country Women's Association of India. The local *Mahila Samiti* she is involved with is engaged in running of the anganwadi center, weaving, and handloom. Besides these, they work as a pressure group in the time when army takes the men in custody. Most of the time, these women go to the army camps and ask for releasing of the suspect, if needed they sit for *Dharna* (demonstration). Ms. Sonowal shared that Army Regiments like Gorkha Regiment is very helpful and people friendly unlike Bihar Regiment. On a quarterly basis, the army invites them for meetings as they have formed a peace committee. During the meetings, the army enquires if their counter-insurgency operations have troubled them. Also, if they have any suggestions for them.

Regarding the unrest and insurgency problem in the state, she felt that it was mainly unemployment. Earlier the boys went with an aim. She felt that the aim was no more there *"lora bur dubhag hol, xihotor udeshwa beleg hol"* (the boys are divided; nowadays their intentions have changed). While talking about the concept of *'Swadhin Asom'* (Independent Assam), she said *"ihote swadhin hoi ki koribo?"* (What are they going to do if they become independent?). "In the beginning, we had faith in ULFA but not anymore. These boys now make extortion demands even to a small *pan dukani* (beetle nut seller). Is there any conscience left with them? They have just turned into a money-extorting group. Our own people have also become so vindictive that they take help of these boys to avenge personal revenges. Is this called justice? No, I really do not agree or support the concept of *'Swadhin Asom'*. I feel that Assam will extinct with all the demands of various groups of people." *"ximane bhag bhag hobo adin Asom or ashtitva naikia hoi xabo"*.

While talking about the future of the state, Ms. Sonowal said that she did not see a bright future for Assam. She said that *"Asomiya bhasa herai goise, engrazik iman guruto dise"* (Assamese language is dying as more importance is given to the English language).

Regarding ULFA and government's role, she felt that as a group these boys should come together for a talk with the government. The role they have been playing was not for the betterment of our society. In fact, it was very much destructive and there was a need for retrospection for these boys.

Mr. Bankim Ch. Phatowali (52 years) is the founder Secretary of *Tinsukia Sahitya Sabha*, and once served as the President of *'Jatiya Unnayan Parishad'* (which is banned now). At present he is the Principal of Kakopathar Higher Secondary School. He shared his fears and apprehensions as a civil society member. His analysis of the situation showed a great deal of understanding on his part when it came to ULFA and other issues.

While talking about the on going situation in the state he said, "There is a feeling of unrest in our state and law and order is a problem. This is due to lack of proper leadership and lack of trust among the various ethnic groups. Moreover, a search for a separate ethnic identity was also creating an unrest in the state."

Regarding ULFA's *'Swadhin Asom'*, he felt that in the real terms ULFA had not done anything concrete for a 'Swadhin *Asom'*. Except the sovereignty issue, he believed in the other aspect or demands of ULFA. As the central government had been taking away, the lion share of the natural resources of our state, he felt that ULFA's demand were just and correct. According to him, nobody was giving much importance to quality education. People had lost control over themselves, gun culture was thriving, and those issues need immediate attention. Without talks and discussions, it would be impossible to bring stability to this region.

Mr. Phatowali felt that ULFA was going strong because of the unemployment problem and help from foreign countries. While talking about ULFA's popular mass support he felt that it was not there anymore because they themselves had been the violator of human rights. According to him, a poll, result would have shown common people supporting the group no more. In the prevailing scenario's context, the other issues in ULFA's agenda were far more important that needed to be addressed immediately. From the government's side also, a genuine effort to resume talks with the boys should have been initiated. Time had already passed that removal of 'Armed Forces Special Power Act' should have been enacted.

Mr. Surendranath Dahotia (77 years) has been living in Kakopathar throughout his life and now enjoying his retired life. When approached to share his views on the matter he felt that he is too old to comment on the issue. Nevertheless, he shared his views later on. Regarding the prevailing situation, he felt that the unrest in the state was terrifying. It had been a long struggle and becoming a problem for the state. There was an urgent need to solve this problem. He felt that law and order was becoming a serious issue in the state.

According to him the people in Kakopathar had been living a peaceful life *"Amar nu apotti koriboloi ki ase kintu aai lora khinir karone raixe bor kosto paise"* (we do not have anything to complain about. But due to ULFA problem common people are getting harassed). He felt that Kakopathar had been underdeveloped and agriculturally not progressing much. According to him those were the main reasons the boys joining ULFA.

While talking on the concept of '*Swadhin Asom*' he said that he was not at all convinced with the concept. The boys should be able to give reasons to common people to believe their demand for a sovereign Assam. They should come back to the mainstream and find a better solution. According to him, nobody knew the real situation why ULFA was still going strong. It might be due to the support ULFA gained in the early period against its fighting the corruption. He later said that ULFA would not enjoy this support for an indefinite period with the recent killings of the innocent people. It would lead both ULFA and the people of Assam to a total devastation. Time had approached both ULFA and the government for a fruitful discussion. He added that the 'Armed Forces Special Power Act' should be removed immediately as in the name of it countless innocent civilians had been harassed.

Mr. Brinci Neog (36 years) is a full time worker (President, All Assam Moran Student Union) of the union and they are mainly involved with activities like demanding tribal status for the *'Morans'*, educational, political, and economic development of the *'Morans'*. His approach and stand towards the ULFA problem was diplomatic.

According to him, the initial ethnic and political unrest in the state had turned into a law and order problem. The concept of *'Swadhin Asom'* emerged due to the ethnic unrest, the root of which he felt was in the central government's negligence towards the ethnic population. That feeling of being exploited and prevailing corruption in the democratic process had been the two causative factors the boys joining ULFA. He added that ULFA's dream of complete freedom or sovereignty would not be achieved if the people of Assam would not have access to quality education and a healthy work culture in the process to make them self-dependent. Constitutional changes were the need of the hour for actualizing the concept of *'Swadhin Asom'*.

He felt that the future of Assam was in a turmoil that was accompanied by decaying of democracy, more corruption, and globalization. "When there is no food, clothing and roof to stay, people will definitely fight." There was an urgent need to address those basic issues.

According to him, ULFA was going strong because it had been a political problem. This movement had its own base as it came into being with AASU movement. The 1985 Assam Accord was a farce; it was not a logical one. "We still do not have the proper definition of our *Bhumiputras* (sons of the soil)."

He felt that there was a popular mass support for ULFA as they had been successful in making the common people understand the exploitation and negligence people had been facing from the centre.

According to him, the common ethnic population of Assam would suffer if ULFA would not have an explicit policy. If they had a crystal-clear policy then they should come forward for a talk and share it with everyone else.

At this point, the government (both state and centre) should develop a specific plan regarding the insurgency problem in the state. He felt that in the state, the class difference was very high and the government was mainly concentrating on the upper class. Corruption had reached the grass root level and there was an urgent need for curbing the evils from the democratic system.

The issues raised by Mr. Neog had a base and those were the issues the civil society organizations over the years were demanding the Government of India to cater.

Mr. Amulya Khatoniar (61 years), who is a journalist by profession, spoke to me with lot of passion regarding the problem of insurgency in the state. He said that the social system, the disparities in the social system and lack of proper governance were the root causes of all the problems in northeast India. He said that due to lack of proper representation in the national level politics especially in the Lok Sabha, the northeast region remained neglected despite its vast natural resources. Along with those problems came the illegal migration, shrinking land holding and a lack of development, which made a group of people to take up arms leading the region to a devastating situation. Moreover, he felt that this group of boys did not take up arms with any ideology; therefore, they never realized where they went wrong. Sometimes they claimed they followed Jyoti Prashad and sometimes Bishnu Rabha. According to him, Bishnu Rabha's gun was a symbol of his ideological belief and with that gun, he did not dictate his actions. His conscience guided them. However, with these boys the gun guided them. Therefore, they did not realize whom they were killing! In fact, in most of the cases, they had killed those innocent people who neither ruled nor exploited us.

While talking on the concept of *'Swadhin Asom'* he said that to form a sovereign state, the group did not seem to have a proper plan of action and aim. A sovereign state would need resources and capacity to sustain which they were not sure of. Again, we would be under someone unless and until our society and governance would not change. Otherwise, things should have been better for us after the British left as governance system came in the hands of the Indians.

Regarding the law and order situation in the state, he said that until we would have the problem of terrorism this would remain as a problem. The future of Assam would be doomed if the situation remained the same. The seventy five per cent of the population of Assam were not aware of the real problem so it was the moral duty of the learned ones to reach to this section of people. It was high time for the civil society to reach to those people but for that, they would have to move away from the cities and target the rural areas.

Mr. Khatoniar said that there was no mass support left for ULFA however, the supports they were getting earlier were due to various reasons. First, people supported them out of fear, secondly, out of sympathy and thirdly, the whole situation was very stimulating and adventurous for some youths.

According to him, the government had taken a wrong way of solving the issue of insurgency. Deployment of army was not the answer. All the people of Assam were not terrorists. With violence, nothing can be solved. The government should have a policy that was democratic in approach. In the name of the arms Forces Special Power Act, army had been killing innocent people. The word 'Sovereignty' should not be an obstacle for having a talk with those boys. The government had been denying the ULFA problem but everyday, new boys were joining the outfit. There would be no other options than talks.

While talking in this context of media's role he said that the regional media had been trying to sensationalize the issue. It always tried to cash on the Assamese sentiment and at times took it in a wrong direction. At the national level, most of the times they did not have the proper understanding of the situation and they were giving a shallow coverage, which was another reason to believe in the nation's neglecting attitude.

He said, as a journalist he had failed to do anything constructive regarding the ULFA problem in the state.This was due to a fear psychosis (as many journalists have been gunned down in the past) and lack of in-depth understanding of the problem. He admitted of being attacked five times on his life that had left him with no strength to carry on his duty properly.

Mr. Khatoniar's case was the classic example where ULFA had tried to stop the civil society from criticizing them. Like late Kamala Saikia, (journalist) who was murdered by the outfit, Mr. Khatoniar was also attacked when he had raised his doubts about their intentions.

Interviewing **Mr. Babul Ahmed** (40 years) was one of the tough interviews for me. It was heartbreaking to see the pain he was going through. His love and loss in the time of conflict was something, which I hope no one would ever need to go through. At present, Mr. Ahmed is involved with a cultural club in Kakopathar and he is the Vice President of the political party AGP, Tinsukia district.

According to him law and order was a major problem in the state. He lost his wife Wahida (30 years) on 10 February 2006. The couple had an inter-religious love marriage. They met each other through cultural activities and Wahida was an excellent actor. They were together for a period of nine years. He was left with their seven years old daughter and an old mother. On the fateful day, his wife, daughter, and mother were at home. The people of Kakopathar area were out on the street showing their respect for the victim whom the army had killed suspecting to be an extremist. When the commotion started between the common people and army, Wahida closed the doors and windows of the house and three of them waited inside for the commotion to subside. Suddenly the CRPF came and started firing towards their house thinking

ULFA cadres were hiding there. A bullet pierced through Wahida's head and went out hitting one of the walls. She fell on the ground and right away, their daughter realized that something was wrong with her mother. She went out and called the neighbors. Wahida struggled for her life twelve hours in the hospital and finally gave in. He said, "It has been a major shock for us and we were innocent bystanders only. My mother is too old to react to all these and my daughter understands everything and she has become quiet since her mother passed away. Recently when I met with an accident and I was away in the hospital, when I came back home my daughter asked me if I was also going away like her mother! She never cried and hardly talks about her mother, my daughter is suffering silently."

He shared that the government announced a compensation of three lakhs rupees but he refused to accept it, as it would not serve any purpose for him. That money would not bring back his wife or their little daughter's mother. In fact, he had already served two months in jail for being felicitated by ULFA for not accepting the government's help.

While sharing his concept of '*Swadhin Asom*' he said that it was not out of context then. In addition, he said he believed in it as the history of Assam says so. He felt that there was a quest for freedom among the youth from the outsiders who were exploiting Assam.

According to him, ULFA was going strong because of the people who had been wanting a sovereign state. The popular mass support was very much there for ULFA. People may not say things out of fear but those who were exploited had a strong support for ULFA. He said that he supported scarifies made by the boys but he did not support the killings of the innocent people, which had been taking place then.

Mr. Ahmed opined that if there were no political will, the common people would suffer more. "Nothing would happen to the capitalist!" Talks and discussion were the only way out from the prevailing situation as it was a political problem.

The government should have a talk without any conditions. Moreover, there was no need for the 'Armed Forces Special Power Act' to dominate the freedom loving people of Assam.

Though Mr. Ahmed lost his beloved wife, he did not lose his faith in ULFA. He believed that the Central Government was still exploiting Assam.

Mr. Nikhishwar Saikia (33 years) is a full time worker of Sauda Asom Motok Yuva Chatra Sanmilan. They are mainly involved with development of Tinsukia district, educational development of the children and demanding six legislative assembly seats for Motoks. Moreover, they are demanding government's special attention to Motok community.

According to him, the law and order was a problem in the state. The unrest and insurgency had been prevailing because the government failed to control it and there was no sincere effort to do something about the poor state of affairs.

He viewed that there was no lucid picture of the concept of a *'Swadhin Asom'* and it was difficult for him to comment on it, as the whole concept itself was confusing.

Regarding the future of Assam, he could not see much change, but according to him in the interior places, the use of *'kani'* (Opium) had declined which was widespread a few years back and people had become united to an extent. He felt that it was high time to take steps for a better future.

While sharing his views on the counterinsurgency measures in the state, he said that ULFA was going strong because there was a lack of sincerity among the army and the government.

He felt that there was a popular mass support for ULFA. It was because he could see about 2000- 2500 people in a funeral of one ULFA member gathering in Sadiya, paying respect for the deceased until the last year.

Retrospecting the prevailing scenario, he felt that it was not a wise decision on the part of ULFA to skip talks on the ground of sovereignty issue and the same applied for the government.

According to him, the 'Armed Forces Special Power Act' had no meaning in Assam as it has failed to curb insurgency in the state. It was merely an instrument to harass the common people and that was the actual situation on the ground.

Mr. Pulok Gohain (31 years), is a full time worker of AASU (Information Secretary, Central Committee), has been involved with AASU since 1990. While interviewing Mr. Gohain I had a lot of discussions and arguments regarding the role of AASU, which at times dictates Assamese women's role and cultural identity. This was stimulating and taken by him with good humor. Regarding AASU's work, he shared that as a student body they were involved with various activities. They were working on an academic calendar for the primary to university students, changes in the syllabus of VIII to XII standards, besides addressing the regional problems of Assam, cultural activism in terms of stopping the next generation from the cultural invasion of pubs and discos, their dress codes etc. Another wing of the body called Assam Unnoti Sena was involved with the cultivation of Papaya in seventy five bighas of land at Tinsukia district. They had already signed the memorandum of understanding with Nilon's company for selling the papayas for making pickles. A total of forty-five girls and boys were involved with it. He said, "When we (Assamese people) compare ourselves with the rest of the country, we are really underdeveloped. For a better future, we need to change the psychology and attitude of the people. There is an urgent need for change in the work culture of the state. Here, for everything we have a *bandh*. Our union has stopped the *bandh* culture for the last five years or so. There is an urgent need for preserving our culture. During our festivals, we should wear our traditional attire. In the day-to-day life, it is not possible but during festivals, at least we should wear our traditional cloths (we are not dictating women to wear traditional cloths but they should maintain their *salinota* (decorum or decency)."

While answering to a question he said that their organization was sustaining through the donations of well-wishers.

On the subject of the insurgency problem in the state, he said, it was because of the exploitation of the central government both economically and politically. The center had not given any importance to the democratic movements. Untill then 'Assam Accord' had not been utilized properly. *"Amak sodai domon kori ahise"* (we have always been subjugated).

He shared that law and order was a problem in the state and the government was responsible for it, *"sorkare aii bisoye kunu dhoronor mon kan nidiye"* (lack of concern on their part).

While viewing his concept on *'Swadhin Asom'* he said that as an organization, they did not believe or acknowledge the concept of it. He said, "We are a democratic organization therefore we think that the issue of *'Swadhin Asom'* should be solved democratically. The government needs appropriate leadership and concern to solve this issue."

While talking about the future of the state, he shared that in future, Assam would face challenges in terms of its quality of education compared to the rest of India. It would also face challenges related to a lack of development and cultural invasions, which had already made its way through various ways like cloths, discos, celebrating rain dances etc.

He shared that as an organization, AASU supported the grievances of ULFA. However, they did not support the other demands of ULFA. He said, "Lack of respect for democratic process by the government was the reason behind a group of boys going out for an armed struggle to assert their rights." He also clarified that AASU was not helping ULFA at all.

He felt that ULFA would sustain as long as Assam's deep-seated problems would be there. Once our Dibrugarh district was the second highest revenue payers after Mumbai. Now compare Mumbai and Dibrugarh. *"Kii dhoronor unnati hol Mumbai r kehtrot aro amar Dibrugarh akedorei thaki gol"* (look at the development stage Mumbai has reached and Dibrugarh remained the same). Counter insurgency measures would not remove ULFA as long as we would have the basic problems in the state.

He felt that discussions and talks without any conditions was the only way out for solving the insurgency problem in the state. Moreover, it should take place with a goodwill and respect. He said, "The ULFA problem is a political problem, our organization supports talks, and in fact, we are demanding it."

He viewed that 'Armed Forces Special Power Act' should be cancelled. "We have organized a North East Students Organization (NESO) seminar for removing this act as it is violating our basic rights."

Mr. Bhaskar Bora (28 years) and **Bipul Neog** (29 years) have just surrendered from ULFA. Both Bhaskar and Bipul came together and they preferred to talk to me together. In fact, Bhaskar did most of the talking as Bipul felt their views were same and he preferred Bhaskar to speak on behalf of him. Throughout the conversation they were edgy as I could gather. They were nervous and later on, I got to know that it was because they had surrendered recently and the other members from the outfit were after their lives. I was hoping that they would not get into any trouble because of me as they came out from their hideouts and were without any security.

After XII standard Bhaskar Bora went to join National Socialist Council of Nagalim (K) before joining ULFA. He worked with Raju Baruah, one of the prominent leaders of ULFA and was involved with arms procurement. He had spent almost eleven years with the organization.

Bipul also went to join the outfit soon after class XII as an underground cadre. Before that, he worked for two to three years overground. He has spent last fifteen years with the organization.

Both Bipul and Bhaskar shared their reason behind joining the organization in the following words *"Atiya ami xi khini matit bohi aso aaikhini amar bupa kokar dinor mati, kintu aikhini xanu amar buli kobo parim. Bahiror manuhe amak suson kori tel, chah aru koyla atiyao ni ase ami ki paisu? Samanyo asukh ata hole ami sikitsar karone hahakar kori thakibo lage, iyat akhon bhal hospital nai". "Aiya suson nohole nu ki"? "Amak amar moulik adhikar samuhor pora banchita korise"* (We are deprived of our basic rights, believing, and experiencing that we went to join the organization. If you look around, all these lands, belonged to our ancestors. Now it is belonged to someone else. They (the outsiders) are still taking away the oil, tea, coal from our lands. In return, what are we receiving? Here we do not even have a proper hospital. Is it not an exploitation? They are depriving us from our basic rights and resources. *"Kintu aii somyoshya samuh sesh huwa nai aro sei karone ami khubei hotash hoisu"* (But unfortunately these problems are not solved yet. We do not see any changes in this regard and that is why we are so disillusioned).

Both of them thought that law and order was a problem in the state. They believed in the complete sovereignty of the state. This belief was very important for them but they were disillusioned at the means of achieving it. "The things turned out not to our expectations and we decided to quit the organization. It was the central leader's group thinking we did not believe any more. The leaders have lost their vision and mission. They are simply killing innocent people and have turned ULFA into a terrorist organization. This is not going to serve for the greater purpose of a '*Swadhin Asom*'.

Regarding ULFA's popular mass support, they said, "It will fade away from the minds of our people. The outfit will not have any say among the common people if it goes on like this. It is not going strong anymore at present with only five hundred or so cadres. They will only survive for a few more years. We do not think there is a popular support left anymore. Moreover, if it is there, it is either due to the fear of the gun or the lure of easy money. Now the policy of ULFA is that they give a lot of money to the youngsters to deliver message or throw a hand grenade. So for a young boy who lives in a rural or semi-rural area, this flow of cash is very lucrative. Earlier, when we used to recruit a boy for the organization, we used to look for all positive and negative attributes of the cadre, his fortitude, and integrity. We used to make the boy work for us overground for a minimum two years and then take them for underground activities or any kind of training, but now the whole concept has changed. Now the organization takes boys who do not have any inspiration of the concept of a *'Swadhin Asom'*. The new breed of boys have not seen the constitution of the organization since the Bhutan camp was closed down. The boys have not even seen the *'Samorik Upobidhi'* (byelaws). So how will the organization function when it does not have any clear-cut design? The leaders are sitting somewhere else and they do not know what is happening in the field. The *'Kajyakori Parishad'* (Executive Council) has not been formed since 2003. We did not like the way we were asked to carry out orders, which were against our morals, and at the same time, we could not question back for being a solider!"

The interview with **Mr. Ranjit Dohotia** (31 years) was quite challenging as he found my research study a city girl's endeavor who did not understand a single thing of the current situation. Nevertheless, it was an interesting interview, where he came up with a lot of convictions regarding his views on the insurgency problem.

Presently Mr. Dohutia is the Joint Secretary of AJYCP. It is mainly involved with various issues concerning Assam.

Some of the main issues they are focusing are on dual citizenship and inner line permit in the state.

He said that the unrest and insurgency problem was the outcome of the people's dissatisfaction with the governance where our basic rights were violated.

While talking about the law and order situation in the state he felt that there had been no such problem. "The Treaty of Yandaboo made us a part of India; otherwise, we were an independent state. There is a relevance of a *'Swadhin Asom'*. "There was no use of opposing ULFA", he said. "Both personally and professionally, I believe in a total autonomy."

Speaking on ULFA and their demand for a sovereign state, he said, *'Swadhin Asom'* concept has its own relevance. "Why should we be part of a country when we were never been part of it except when few unfaithful people dragged the British to solve our disputes? People are scared to support ULFA openly but given an opportunity the people of Assam will run to join ULFA."

He felt that ULFA was going strong despite counter-insurgency in the state due to the popular mass support it was gaining.

While talking about ULFA's role in the prevailing situation he said he did not have any suggestions or comments for ULFA. "There are many myths that ISI of Pakistan or Bangladeshi government is helping ULFA. What about the grenades discovered which were made in China? Because the government of India can boss around with the Bangladesh and Pakistan, they are being accused of helping ULFA, but why the government does not have a say about all these Chinese involvement? It is high time that the Government of India should come forward for an unconditional talk with ULFA and solve the issue."

Ms. Ranjana Chetia Phukan (33 years) is a homemaker at present. She is the spouse of Jibon Moran, one of the oldest members of ULFA, Kakopathar. Ranjana is a tough beautiful woman who gave her consent to be interviewed but interviewing Ranjana was one of the frustrating experiences of my field study. She was apprehensive of talking to me without taking permission from her husband, who was one of the prominent leaders, of ULFA and away in a foreign country. They have two grown up daughters, and it is for the sake of her daughters' education she had taken retirement from the outfit. In fact she had stayed in jail for a few months and now out on bail. Throughout her interview, she gave non-committal answers, which made me, wonder how she landed up with the organization which demand for a sovereign state. At times, she refused to give any answers to my queries. The excerpts of the interview are as below.

While talking about the unrest and insurgency problem in the state she said that it was all because of the exploitation of the central government. She felt that there was a law and order problem in the state.

She said that she supported and believed in the concept of a *'Swadhin Asom'*. Nevertheless, she could not justify her belief with a sound reasoning.

She felt that ULFA was sustaining so long because of the support of the common people. One section of the society wants ULFA to be there. It is because of the neglect of the government of India towards the people of Assam. "During the election time the representatives come and campaign and once the election is over they forget these common people who select them."

Regarding ULFA's role, she felt that the outfit should come forward for the talk but with their conditions.

According to her, the government should come for the talk without any conditions (*Malike ba akou ki koi*...wondering what the answer of her husband would be!). Regarding the 'Armed Forces Special Power Act', she felt that it needed to be abolished but she was doubtful regarding government's intentions.

Ms. Parul Sarma (80 years) is a retired teacher and full time writer. She is also the President of Tinsukia Sahitya Sabha and Law College.

It was another Assam *bandh* the day I went to meet Ms. Sarma, she was waiting near the gate of her residence when I walked to her place along with my friend Pranab in Tinsukia. Ms. Sarma lives separately in the part house, which she shares, with her son and daughter-in-law. Her sitting room is full of various certificates, awards showing part of her contribution to the society. When I introduced myself, she told me that in one of her novel a character's name was Prateeti. She made tea for us and read out one of her poems inspired by ULFA in their heydays. She amazed me with her love for life and commitment towards the society. The excerpts of our discussion are as follows.

While talking about the insurgency problem in the state she said, "One needs to worry about the present situation. This unrest is due to lack of trust among us. These days, emotions and feelings like love and affection have vanished from our society. People have become self-centered. When the basic values of the society melt away, it creates a situation like this."

Regarding the ULFA problem, she said, "In the beginning I believed that something will change because of these boys. During the Assam Movement, I was jailed and beaten up by the army. In fact, my left ear is completely deaf due to that beating. My family had to deposit ninety five thousand rupees for my bailout in 1980. Therefore, when these boys came out, I really believed their concept of a *'Swadhin Asom'* but not anymore. What have they turned into now?" "*Nixor aiijonik sukhot rakhiboli anor ghorot thakile hobo xanu?Nixe nixor deshot thaki swabolombi houk* (to keep your mother happy will you stay in somebody else's house? They have to become self sufficient in their own country and not in some other's). They have been destroying everything we had here. What is the use? Have they ever done anything good for themselves?

They should be able to convince the centre through proper means, not like this, it is not going to bring about any change."

Ms. Sarma felt that the boys did not enjoy the popular mass support once they used to. It was happening because the path they had chosen. She said that both the government of India and ULFA need to think of talks seriously otherwise we would face more disaster.

Mr. Bikul Baruah (40 years) is the younger brother of ULFA leader Paresh Baruah. He is a teacher in Jerai primary school. He spoke to us when we were waiting for his mother to be interviewed. To enter Jerai, I had to get through a troop of army men, who searched the car and people who accompanied me. After scanning my identity card and the reason behind my visit, they allowed me to go ahead. I went to Jerai to meet Mrs. Miliki Baruah, mother of Paresh Baruah. The drawing room of Mrs. Baruah adorns the photograph of Paresh and his late elder brother along with some toy guns in the showcase. After reaching the residence, we waited for her about one and half hours but at the end she declined to be interviewed. So while waiting for her, I had a chance to talk to Bikul Baruah and his wife. Regarding the insurgency problem in the state Mr. Baruah had to say the following.

> "They have been fighting for last thirty years; if they come back without a *'Swadhin Asom'* the people of Assam will not forgive them as so many boys have died for the cause. They should get what they have been fighting for *"Kheti korile tar phol paboi lagibo"*. We may not get a complete sovereign state but like Nagaland, any outsider coming to Assam should not have the right to purchase any landed property here. If they buy also it has to be in the name of some Assamese people. Unemployment, frustration are the reasons for the whole situation. The mindset of the people has to change from job orientation to something

different. Even the treatment and attitude of the government towards SULFA is also wrong and many boys have taken the path of arms coming back to the mainstream to make money by using their muscle power. The government is also using them."

Mr. Gaurikanta Gohain (55 years) is an Office Assistant in a Tea Garden and his daughter **Barnali Gohain** (26 years) is pursuing her PhD in Assam Agricultural University, Jorhat. The father daughter had a different stand on the issue of ULFA.

Mr. Gohain felt that when ULFA was formed initially it had a different agenda. They were not into the killing or extortion but they were only for the development of the region. He said *"Aami ane ata porjayoloi namim buli ketiyao bhoba nasilo* (we never thought we will reach in such a situation)."

While talking about the prevailing situation he felt that it was due to the failure of the government's policy. He lamented, "Assam has given so much of raw materials to the country, but when it comes to giving something back to Assam, the government has always failed to do so. Every year with the natural disasters we are losing so many lives and land (due to erosion)." He added, "Unemployment is the main causes of this problem. Our boys are educated but there is no job prospect for them. I have a job, I work in my field, and that is how I am educating my five children. However, I do not know whether they will get any job in future. Besides unemployment, unequal distribution of resources is another reason why boys are joining ULFA. Look at our region (upper Assam) which is not as developed as compared to lower Assam. Jorhat has the Engineering College, Agricultural University. The Secretariat of Assam has only people from the Lower Assam; I could not find there a single person from the '*Moran-Matak*' origin." He said, "The *Moran-Matak* people are originally backward and they are still the same, which needs more attention, developmental measures and there should be an equal distribution of resources."

He further added, "We want ULFA and government both to come for a talk where they discuss the basic issues concerning the state and these issues should be acceptable for us. When PCG came, we had a lot of hope but it did not materialize. There are certain issues like corruption for which we look forward to ULFA to take some action against it. If we try to speak against corruption, people involved with it will kill us, and to go to the police is a wastage of time and energy. Again, if we say we need ULFA it will be another problem. Nevertheless, we need a peaceful solution to all our problems. I do not support killing of innocent people but there are certain causes, which are still valid. If the government does not address the basic issues of the state, there will be more ULFA in future. We need to have proper industrial policies and employment opportunities for our youth."

He felt that though there was no explicit support to ULFA from the mass but covertly people still supported them. In addition, he felt that the government needed to remove the 'Armed Forces Special Power Act' as it was not a democratic way of dealing the situation. This Act was violating our basic human rights.

On the other hand, **Barnali Gohain** said that she did not believe ULFA and their cause. She said, "Violence is not going to bring anything. People need to develop themselves and find out what is stored for them. People here are not at all aware and it is due to their own lacking. If they do not venture out how will they know? I do not support this violent path and it is not going to bring us anything."

She further added, "There may be a hidden support for ULFA, but not openly any more as it was earlier. I belong to this place but I do not support them."

Looking into the on going situation, she felt that the future of Assam would look brighter in terms of the Look East Policy, which according to her will open up northeastern states with the rest of the southeast asian countries.

She further said that the government of India and ULFA need to come for a talk to solve this long-standing problem. Moreover, the government would need to remove the 'Armed Forces Special Power Act' as soon as possible.

Mr. Brahma Dutta Mahanta (73 years) and **Ms. Thuluki Mahanta** (68 years) are the proud parents of late Anil Mahanta, an ULFA cadre. Anil Mahanta died in an encounter in Kampur, Nagaon in the year 1997. The family did not bring the dead body to Kakopathar and he was cremated in Kampur.

The parents knew that he was involved with ULFA from the beginning and they were proud of their son. Both said *"xe desor karone gol, ami tar karone gorbo koru"* (he died for his country and we are proud of him). They said, "Yes we do miss him but we have sacrificed him for the cause of the country which is far greater than anything. We do believe in the cause of ULFA and we have sacrificed our son for that cause".

Shri Chakreshwar Mahanta (61 years) is a Vaishnavite priest of Shri Shri Mayamora Hatigad Mulani Satra (Tipuk), which is situated at Kakopathar. He has ten to twelve thousand disciples at present.

Regarding the ULFA problem particularly in Kakopathar area, he felt that it was due to the 'feeling of alienation' among the people of that area. He said that when the tea garden stared growing, people moved to the more interior places and gradually the land holding got smaller due to that increase in population. In that process, the people stared feeling being deprived of their rights and thus took up arms to get back their rights. Another reason he felt was that Kakopathar had been close to Arunachal Pradesh, which helped the boys to move freely in that area. Nevertheless, mainly it was the feeling of alienation among the people, which was the prime cause of the ULFA problem.

He said that it was high time that both ULFA and the government needed to come forward and have a talk, otherwise lot of innocent people would be killed.

The analysis of Shri Mahanta showed the actual feeling of the people of Kakopathar. The feeling of exploitation and alienation based on geographical locations were some of the reasons boys joining the outfit from this part of the state.

I depended on my luck and went to meet one of the 'boys' to have a talk in the evening in Kakopathar. It was in an interior village. On the way we were given instructions as which route to take and ask the villagers for a particular house where our meeting was fixed. When we reached, we were ushered to the room of a typical village house with a happy family where the grandfather was holding his grandchild. I was a bit apprehensive thinking if the army comes then what would happen to that family. Nothing of that short happened. On our way, we met three convoys of army, but no one questioned us. There were around four boys including **Joon Bhuyan** (approximately 26/27 years) who sat in the room and three more who stood guarding the house. Except Joon all other boys were armed with AK 47. We were told Joon and his band of boys came walking almost three hours from their hideouts for the interview.

After my introduction and objectives of my study, I got the chance of talking to Joon who is a self-styled Sergeant Major of ULFA, about his mission and the organization. He said that they believed in the concept of a *'Swadhin Asom'*. Sovereignty was what they had been demanding and fighting for all the years. When asked about their plan of action if they achieve sovereignty, he said, their immediate action would be a general consensus open to all the people of Assam of their choice to stay with ULFA or not. "It is not that we do not want peace, in fact, we would like to go for talks with the government of India but of course not without any conditions." While talking about killing innocent people citing the Dhemaji incident (where many schoolchildren were killed) he defended that they asked the people not to come out that day but they did not listen. It was government's failure that it could not protect those people. He said, *"Amak jonosadharone atiyo bhal pai aro biswas kore seibabei ami aso* (common people still love and trust us and that is why we are still sustaining)."

Before leaving, the boys who accompanied Joon shook hands with us and said, *"Log pai bhal lagil Baideo"* (it was nice meeting you elder sister). I had the chance of looking at them from a close quarter and it broke my heart to see such young boys have taken to a path, which was so violent. I just prayed that one day I would meet them again in a safer environment without their guns. While coming back home our car broke down thrice and they enquired again, whether we have reached home safe.

[P.S. In June 2008, Joon Bhuyan along with Mrinal Hazarika and Jiten Dutta 'A' and 'C' company of 28th Battalion of ULFA came overground with their desire to talk and called for a ceasefire with the Government of India.]

II

Dr. J. K. Mahanta (55 years) and his wife both are into teaching and both preferred to write their views rather than discussing it. The extract of their writings are as follows.

Regarding the law and order situation in the state he said, "I do not think that the law and order is a problem in the state at this moment."

According to him, the concept of a *'Swadhin Asom'* is far from reality and feasibility and he did not support the concept. "It would be obvious that the state of Assam cannot sustain its sovereignty without the support or help from its greater part i.e. Indian territory. It would be foolish to cherish the concept with the available resources of the state. Yes, I do see changes that lately people begin to think in this context. Majority of the populace of our state think that Assam can not be a sovereign country with the social, political, and economic limitations."

He said, "The future of Assam looks gloomy and perplexing. Power of an organization rests on its mass support and not on the scattered misanthropic activities. I do not think there is a popular mass support left for ULFA. The news items published every now and then is sufficient to explain the fact that the organization is loosing its mass support gradually. If the organization resurrects overground to lead the people to fight for injustice done to them or if the organization comes forward to the development of the down trodden, they would have been more popular and this mission would have been a more effective one."

He added further, "Being impartial to everybody the government must maintain law and order and come forward to have a discussion regarding grievances of the insurgents. The 'Armed Forces Special Power Act' should not be in force."

Dr. Junu Mahanta (50 years) said, "I am a member of a women's organization and we are mainly involved with activities like legal awareness, health awareness and creating a platform for creative work."

According to her, she did not think there was any law and order problem in the state. She said, "The concept of a *'Swadhin Asom'* is based on emotion rather than reasons. I do not support the concept of *'Swadhin Asom'*. In the context of globalization, granting of sovereignty to a small state like Assam is detrimental to the development of the state. And most of the people do not support the concept."

She added, "I feel the future of Assam is very gloomy and problematic. Any organization's permanency depends on the public support and everything should be according to reasons without doing harm to the innocent people. In the struggle for sovereignty, they must not make the innocents suffer. They should try to understand what actually the impression of the general public is."

According to her, the Government should come forward to have an unconditional discussion with the insurgents with an open mind so that the people of Assam can live in peace and amity. The 'Arms Forces Special Power Act' should be abolished as it caused mistrust and sometimes lead the people in power to misuse it.

Interviewing **Jatindra Nath Neog,** (65 years) made me remember the genuine teachers who taught and groomed us to be responsible and contributing citizens of the country. I could feel the level of his frustration regarding the next generation of teacher and student, both lacking the dedication in this trade.

Presently Jatindra Nath Neog is involved with Chabua Jestha Nagarik Santha (Secretary), Chabua Sahitya Sabha (Advisor, involved with it for last 30 years), and Sauda Asom Motok Sanmilan (Executive Member). He is mainly looking into the issues like HIV/AIDS, Guthkha addiction etc. He is also involved with literary activities and gives voluntary tuitions to poor students on a regular basis.

Mr. Neog said that the problem of insurgency was different in different places. Unemployment as pointed out by many was not the only cause of insurgency according to him. Easy money, exposure to violence, movies, gun culture, people's instigation at times were also some of the reasons which were leading the boys to join insurgent groups. The political and social systems failed to utilize and capture the youth power. *Aru Jatigoto bhabe Asomiya poriyale lora suwalik mulyobodh dibo nuwarile* (Assamese families have failed to inculcate values to their children). "I feel the psychology of the people of Assam has changed so much in the recent years. During our times, we had a sense of duty and gave our services to the needy ones and to the society. But the whole concept of doing something for your society has taken over by selfish attitudes. Nowadays, the teachers themselves are involved in corruption. What education or moral value are they going to impart to the students! The human emotions like love, compassion, tolerance, sympathy, and empathy have vanished from our society. There were mistakes in the past but now if all the intellectuals of Assam come forward and take some concrete steps then we may correct these for a better future."

While talking about ULFA's *'Swadhin Asom'*, he said he did not support it at all. He concluded, "They could have done something constructive with all the money, time, and energy they had wasted till now."

He felt that ULFA was going strong despite counter insurgency measures, as in the hearts of the people they were still alive. However, at the same time he did not think ULFA still had that popular mass support because they had disappointed the same people. "Once upon a time ULFA was involved with certain social activism but now they have turned into something else."

He adds further, "Except the sovereignty demand, ULFA now should try fulfilling their other demands." Regarding the 'Armed Forces Special Power Act', he said, "If the terrorist kill more than the army what will happen to our people? We are feeling safe because of this act."

Ms. Jyoti Hazarika (40 years) is the mother of late ULFA militant Sameer Hazarika, alias Raju Hazarika. His body was found near a bridge in Dibrugarh in year 2000, 22 December. He was shot from a close range on the head and chest. Nobody knew who or why he was killed except that he was then a member of the outfit.

Sameer was the second of the three siblings. Jyoti Hazarika lost her husband in the year 1987 when Sameer was six, his elder brother was seven and sister was just one year old. Jyoti was given a job in the ONGC on a compensatory ground where her husband worked. She left Sameer with his paternal uncle and aunt as it was difficult for her to look after three kids all alone. When asked whether she had any idea of Sameer's plan of joining the outfit she said that she did not know anything as she was staying away from him. But his aunt challenged (who was also present during the interview) Jyoti and asked her to give the real answer to the question. Jyoti again said that Sameer was very unhappy with his mother. He was so unhappy and disillusioned that soon after his matriculation examination he left the house to join ULFA. Till his death he never tried to come back home.

Nevertheless, the aunt (Gayatri Hazarika) who brought Sameer up felt proud of him and felt that ULFA was doing a commendable job for the betterment of the society.

The rest of the conversation did not go further as there was tension brewing up between Jyoti and Gayatri. In fact, Jyoti refused to talk further as she felt that Sameer's aunt always blamed her for Sameer's death.

When **Mr. Kumbheswar Hazarika** (47 years) alias **Billu Saikia** walked into the room, I could gather that it was physically painful for him to walk properly. His speech was blurred and he looked much older than fourty seven years. Looking at him and his mother made me feel sad. The old mother was telling me *"mor lora tu xe basi ase aaijoxoni seyai bohut" atiya tak bohut bhalole anilu" "Xe mora ne xia aku dhoribo nuwara abosta hoisil"* (he was almost dead, now he looks much better and thank goodness that my son is still alive). All these happened when the Indian army captured him. He was tortured with all the third degree measures like electric shocks, beating, plucking of his nails etc.

Kumbheshwar Hazarika went to join ULFA in the year 1979. He was trained in Myanmar, and during the Bajrang operation, he was caught in a nursing home in Guwahati, where he was admitted for Malaria and other ailments. He was detained in Dinjan camp of Dibrugarh. As he did not cooperate with the army, he was handed over to the family.

Looking into the health status of Mr. Hazarika the outfit relieved him from all his duties, so he was a retired member of ULFA not a surrendered ULFA. He and his family members were proud of his contribution for the country. Kumbheshwar said of himself as *"mor jibon tu sesh hoi gol Ulfa ar karone aro mor kunu aakhep nai"* (I have sacrificed my life for ULFA and I do not have any regrets).

Looking into the ongoing situation Kmbheswar Hazarika felt that both ULFA and government of India needed to come forward for talks.

Meeting **Ms. Gitimoni Gogoi Hazarika** (23 years), her toddler son and her mother Kunjalata Gogoi was a heart breaking experience. Gitimoni is the widow of late Kamal Hazarika alias Bagh alias Hirokjyoti Hazarika. Kamal Hazarika was a surrendered ULFA. Kamal surrendered in the year 1999 and he was gunned down by ULFA in the year 2006 on 18 October. Kamal was running a small roadside *Dhaba* (eatery). He was killed because ULFA thought he was a police informer. In fact, Gitimoni said that his life was made miserable by the army, as they would pick him up anytime with them to track the other ULFA caders.

Gitimoni was married for five and half years. Their son was just three months old when Kamal died. After his death, Gitimoni's in laws have severed their relationship with her and her son. They also have told her that she had no claims to the ancestral property of Kamal, though it was an arranged marriage fixed by their respective parents.

Throughout our conversation, Kunjalta kept breaking down and Gitimoni kept holding back her tears. She told me *"Baideo mor sokupani sukai goise, kiman kandim aro"* (elder sister, how much will I cry? My tears have dried down). Kunjalata herself lost her husband at a very young age and single handedly she brought up her daughter and married her off to Kamal when she just finished her 10th examination. Gitimoni did her graduation after marriage. Kunjalata told me, *"Bhanti tumi xanibai amar somajot bidhowak ki dhorone bebohar kore? Amak dekhile manuhor zatra nasti hoi* (sister you must be aware how painful for a widow to face the society where they are ridiculed by people for bringing ill luck). *Xihote amako mari thoi xabo lagisil, ketiyaba nixie kerosene dhali xolai aiko mari pelam xen lage* (they should have killed us too, sometime I feel like killing her and myself by pouring kerosene). The life of a surrendered member's widower is much more humiliating."

Gitimoni said, "ULFA should have killed all of us because now I am left with nothing even the *dhaba* owned by my husband was also taken away by my in laws." She did not know how to bring up her son after her mother would die. People did not like to help her, as she was a widow of a SULFA who did not live enough to build a proper house. While I was leaving, Gitimoni showed me one particular corner of their compound where they have cremated Kamal. She said, "When our son grows up I will have something to show him of his father."

III

Mr. Zaheer Choudhury (27 years) is a young dedicated social worker who is working in a NGO '*Sauda Asom Pathar Porichalona Samiti*, Nalbari. He spoke earnestly on various issues concerning the problem. Presently he is in the post of the Assistant Secretary of the organization. This organization was formed in the year 1994.

The NGO Zaheer is working are mainly involved in activities related to training agricultural activities, cultivation and liasoning with the companies. This year for the first time, they are entering in the area of sugarcane business where they are working with a private company.

Regarding the insurgency problem in the state, he said that it was very much there. He felt that it was due to the terrorism, and political and economic backwardness in the region.

About ULFA's *'Swadhin Asom'*, he said he believed it and supported the concept from bottom of his heart. He had the feeling that except the voting power, the people of Assam did not have any other rights. They were treated as the secondary citizen by the central government irrespective of their political affiliation. "The boys who are fighting for a *'Swadhin Asom'* are from the farmers' class. People from this class are dying everyday due to exploitation. A farmer for his rights has to ask his son to pick up a gun and fight against the system. If needed one has to fight for her/his rights and take up the gun. The mainland Indians have noticed us since the Assam Movement, and the ULFA issue has made the centre to notice us again. In the initial days, the boys have done some good deeds but later on, they have done a lot of harm to themselves as well as to others. The peasant class has been deprived of their dues for a long time. If the government gives better facilities to them, then we can think of a better future as majority of us belong to this class. Due to the lack of proper facilities, this class of people is not been able to develop itself and it is one of the main reasons of all the problems."

According to him, ULFA was going strong because of the unresolved problems of unemployment, and unequal development in the state.

He also felt that still there was a popular mass support for the organization "We do not want to be a second class citizen. After AASU, ULFA is such an organization which will fight for our rights and *Swadhinota* (freedom)."

Regarding ULFA and government of India's role, he had to say, "At present, ULFA needs to come back to the people of Assam and ask their opinion and support. There were times when ULFA did some grave mistakes. For that, they need to apologize. We want a peaceful environment and ULFA needs to think about this and work for it. The government needs to solve this problem politically. They should accept the sovereignty issue and go ahead with the talks."

He felt that the 'Armed Forces Special Power Act' needed to be abolished as it gave a free hand to the army to pick up any one and kill anyone without explanations.

Mr. Brojen Talukdar (35 years) is a teacher by profession but he prefers to introduce himself as a journalist. There was a time when he was hounded for being pro ULFA. He came up with lot of strong ideas and we had a very lively discussion.

According to him, corruptions, illiteracy, ignorance among the people were the reasons of all the unrest in the state. These lead to anger and frustration among the common people. "People are still sleeping under the open sky. In our own Nalbari district, approximately two hundred people are still living on the embankment of Pagladia River, as they have lost everything in the last decade. Their human rights are violated everyday."

He felt that the law and order was a problem in the state. Especially for a commoner the presence of these security people can be terrifying.

While talking about a *'Swadhin Asom'* he said, "There is no environment for a *'Swadhin Asom'*. Yes, I do believe in the concept of a *'Swadhin Asom'*. I believe in becoming self-reliant not necessarily seceding from the mainland India but we should be able to look after ourselves without any bindings. We do not have the freedom of living in a peaceful country with all these corruption and exploitations. The leaders in Delhi are exploiting the Assamese people. Therefore, we need a *'Swadhin Asom'*. I see changes in terms of attitude of the people in both Dispur and New Delhi. They have recognized ULFA as a powerful organization which speaks for the common people of Assam."

He said, "The future of Assam is very bleak as the way government of India is dealing with the problems in the state. Our education system is so pathetic where we are not groomed properly and we cannot pursue the dream we want.

We do not have any control in our professional life and we end up in jobs which are of no interest to us."

Regarding the mass support towards ULFA, he said, "In the rural areas people still support ULFA. People never consider them as their enemy. Army also has guns but they are not being supported by the common people. The popular mass support is very much there for ULFA. There are villages, which are so far from the main town one cannot imagine unless one goes there. The police do not reach there, and the people definitely depend on these boys. The people there are so poor that they do not even know the use of *'soriyoh tel'* (cooking oil used for making curries and fries). These boys are like god for them who help them out when there is a need. There are people who are without a roof even in our village, which is so near to the highway. There is so much of corruption and exploitation in the society that we need these boys to keep a tab on them. The administration including the army and the police do not want to solve the problem of ULFA. There is the issue of rehabilitation of the surrendered boys and the huge amount of money involved with it. Even during encounters, they can make money. Everybody has got hand in gloves while making money out of this problem."

Speaking on the local media's role he said, "Not only local and regional media has a role to play on issues concerning people but at the same time various civil society organizations, government and even the insurgent organizations have a role to play. We need to give power to the local people. We need a change. We will fight against the system to bring about a change no matter what means we take."

He said that there was an urgent need to remove the 'Armed Forces Special Power Act'. It was violating our basic human rights being one of the infamous acts of our country.

Mr. Syed Tafikur Rahman (33 years) is a member of Asom Jatiyatabadi Yuva Chatra Parishad (AJYCP). According to him, AJYCP is involved with many activities so that there can be a peaceful discussion of the problems in the state besides other demands of the organization.

He felt that apart from the ULFA problem at that moment, we did not have any other serious problem in the state. Under the then government, people were feeling safer to move in the nighttime, which was not so earlier.

Regarding the concept of a *'Swadhin Asom'* he said that as an organization they did not talk of a *'Swadhin Asom'* but they would demand for a *'Self Governance'* where finance, defense, international relationships and communication will be with the center and other aspects should be with the people of Assam to manage. Moreover, personally he did not support the concept of a *'Swadhin Asom'* as it was impossible to achieve it.

Speaking about the future of Assam, he said, "I see changes in terms of youth becoming self reliant, ULFA, and government coming together for a peaceful talk."

While speaking about popular mass support for ULFA he said, "Some boys have joined ULFA emotionally, some have joined due to the unemployment. There is a strong support for ULFA and therefore it is still going strong."

Regarding the role of ULFA and government in solving the insurgency problem in the state, he said, "ULFA needs to come for a peaceful solution and discussion. If they keep asking for a *'Swadhin Asom'*, it is never going to happen, as the government is not going to accept this. The government has to give back something from their side as many young boys have given their blood for this cause."

He further added that the 'Armed Forces Special Power Act' needed to be removed from the state immediately.

Mr. Hemanta Kalita (37 years) is the elder brother of late Basanta Deka alias Anup Deka. Basanta Kalita was in ULFA and he died during a shootout at Myanmar. When I reached Hemanta Kalita's home, he was away for some work in the village. While waiting for him I saw the photograph of Basanta, which was hanging flaccidly on the wall of the drawing room and the certificate the family had received from ULFA for his martyrdom. After initial preliminaries, we had a talk as how Hemanta and his family faced the consequences of Basanta joining the outfit. To survive from the army atrocities Hemanta left for Dibrugarh in the year 1991 as that year Basanta had joined the outfit and that was the year Assam got the first president's rule. That year Hemanta contested gaon panchayat election on behalf of the Congress party but he lost it against the Asom Gana Parishad candidate.

Though he managed to stay away from the army being away in Dibrugarh, the other members of the family were not spared. Their uncle, aunt and cousins were tortured and the army even kept their father in the custody. Hemanta openly never asked his father about any torture lashed upon him but he was sure the Indian army did not spare their father. However, the whole family and their extended family members took the army atrocities on their stride.

Hemanta never had any clue that his brother was joining the outfit. Their age difference was only three years. Basanta somehow did his class XI in Nalbari College and went underground immediately. He died on 17 April, 1995. He was hardly in his twenties. The family never got the dead body of Basanta, as he died in Myanmar. The family got the news of his death through the other boys but never believed it till they received the certificate from ULFA. They even tried locating him in different places but it was without any success.

When asked whether Hemanta ever tried to bring back his younger brother, he told that for Basanta the cause and the country were more important than his family. When Basanta went to join ULFA, both Hemanta and his father, who was alive at that time felt proud. Even after his death, the pride remained the same "*xi deshor karone gol* (he went for the country)!"

Hemanta said, "My brother died for ULFA. I want ULFA to continue with their works but I do not support the killings of the innocent people who have not done anything to harm the organization. Punishing someone who has done wrong for the outfit is justified. If they want to come for talks, I will support it. As for now, everyone wants to live in a peaceful state and therefore both the government of India and ULFA should come for a talk. Nevertheless, our demands need to be fulfilled. If needed sovereignty also. If we became sovereign, we will be proud as an '*Asomiy Jati*' which includes everyone who has the voting right in the country."

When asked whether he felt himself to be living under anyone he said, "I am a citizen of a sovereign country!"

I went to meet **Mr. Brojen Choudhury** (31 years) in his AJYCP office in Nalbari town. He took a lot of interest in my study and even helped me to find some other participants. Brojen is a dedicated worker of the organization and we had a long discussion at different points of time regarding the insurgency problem in the state.

Brojen has been involved with AJYCP for the last four years. Presently he is the President of the district committee of the organization. Besides their four major demands locally, the group is involved with various developmental works in the district.

Regarding the insurgency problem in the state he said, "I do not think insurgency and unrest is a problem but the dissatisfaction of not getting our basic rights is the main problem. We are not the actual owner of our resources. We have some basic problems like flood, lack of communication system, problem of the immigrants that have never been addressed properly. The current law and order problem cannot be improved with the deployment of Indian Army."

About the concept of a '*Swadhin Asom*' he said, "As an organization we do not support the concept of a '*Swadhin Asom*'. We give importance to *Jatiya Puji Gathan*. We believe in *Sangram* not *Andolan*. ULFA's concept of a '*Swadhin Asom*' is not addressing the economic aspect of our state. Nothing has changed so far. Those who are representing us are not voicing the actual demands of the state. The overall situation is not very bright. The demands made by ULFA legitimize in a way if you give a closer look to the problems of the state."

He said that in the interior places people still believed what ULFA was saying. The common people supported them especially at the village level that was why they had been still surviving.

He added, "Now both the government and ULFA should come for a talk. As an organization, on 9 December, 2000 we had a meeting in Bagamati near Bhutan border asking ULFA to leave the violent path and come for a peaceful solution."

Interviewing **Mr. Divya Jyoti Haloi** (29 years) lead us to a lengthy discussion regarding the insurgency problem in the state. Although Divya Jyoti represented the Youth Congress (District General Secretary) most of the times, he asked me to consider all his views as a personal than an organizational one.

Regarding the insurgency problem in the state he said, "I do not think it is a problem. It is just a part of an evolution. There will be always oppressor and oppressed and a conflict will be a part of the society." He added that the psychology of our youth was that they wanted the best of everything without the realization whether they were capable of doing the hard work, which would be required to achieve success in life. By dreaming or asking, one would not get things done. It would require sheer hard work and determination. "If you are not competent enough then there will be always a problem."

He felt that the law and order situation was far better during the then government (Congress). While speaking about believing the concept of a '*Swadhin Asom*', he said, "I do not believe in the concept because I feel proud when I introduce myself as an Indian. If we become a sovereign state, then I do not think we will feel that strength as we are feeling being an Indian now. If the people of Assam do not try to solve this issue immediately, it will remain as a problem forever."

He felt that the future of Assam would look brighter as the youth had become aware that they could not solely depend on jobs any more. But at the same times he was apprehensive of the way illegal migration was taking place in the state.

He said that ULFA did not enjoy the popular mass support it used to get earlier as people had lost their trust in them. It was high time that the government should try to bring back those boys. Most of the cases the boys who had joined the outfit were out of absolute frustration, there was no ideological attachment. Therefore, both the government and ULFA should come forward for a talk as soon as possible.

Divya Jyoti felt that the 'Armed Forces Special Power Act' was needed in the state. He said, "Otherwise we would have the hooligans extorting money in the name of various outfits."

Ms. Sewali Baruah (17 years) and **Ms. Jyotika Kalita** (17 years)[1] came to meet me in the AJYCP office to share their views on the insurgency problem in the state. Both Sewali and Jyotika have passed their XII standard from Assam Valley Academy Junior College, Nalbari.

They felt sad when they saw the kind of activities ULFA was involved with. They said, "In the past ULFA must have done something good but not anymore, they are killing the innocent people now." They felt that unemployment was the main reason behind boys joining ULFA.

Both said that the government needed to solve the problem peacefully. They added *"Bortoman Asomot kiman samshya ase ULFA aro sorkar log hoi aai samoshya bor somadhan kora usit nohole bhobishyote aro saamoshya barhi xabo"* (We have enough problems in the state now which both ULFA and the government should work together to solve before they become too much to tackle with).

When I walked into **Ms. Nalini Baruah's** (57 years) residence she looked very harassed and absent minded. Throughout our conversation, she was holding back her tears. There were moments when we could not talk any more. It was a painful experience for both us to think and talk of a dead seventeen years old boy. She is not only the mother of late Azad Jyoti Baruah but also the wife of famous actor, director, and play writer Bhaben Baruah. Before her marriage, Nalini was an accomplished theater actor, but after her marriage, she had to leave everything and become a full time homemaker. Her married life was full of troubles as it was an inter caste marriage (she is a Brahmin and husband was from Kayastha caste) and at the same time she was an actor in those days.

Nalini and late Bhaben Baruah's first child Azad Jyoti Baruah joined ULFA when he was studying in class XII. Nalini Baruah said, "As parents we tried our best to bring him back. In fact, few days before his death he came home and asked his father to go and talk to his colleagues so that he can come home and appear for his XII examination. Unfortunately, those concerned colleagues did not allow him to comeback. Ironically, those boys within a few days after his death, surrendered and took retirement from the organization. When I met them later I asked them what happened to those tall claims they made when this young boy who was just seventeen years old wanted to come back from a violent path."

Nalini said, "Azad was an inquisitive and sensitive child. He used to write poems, recite, and was involved with theater. He was sensitive to people who were needy. He would often come and tell me about the way people treated those small children as domestic helps. He would give away things to people without thinking twice. He loved to help the people who were marginalized. I am not surprised the way he died and the path he chose. *"aaji xe mori bohutok bosai thoi goise nohole tar hatot bahut manoh morile hoi"* (it's a blessing that he died otherwise someone else would have died in his hands). He has seen a lot of social and family abuse towards me. In fact, he was ridiculed for the color of his skin. All these things troubled him a lot. I never got a chance to talk to him properly, may be things would have been different for us if I had the chance!"

Nalini said, *"prothom abostat Azad a 'Swadhin Asom', or sopun tuk biswas korisil, kintu tar pasoloi muhobhabga hol"* (In the beginning Azad believed the concept of sovereignty but later on he was completely disillusioned with it)." Regarding Nalini's belief in the concept of a *'Swadhin Asom'*, she said, she never had believed in it and neither her husband. She said, *"amar manuhor majot akota khub kom, sei karone biswas tu nasil, aaji tumi moi kotha patisu kaliloi ami dorkar hole uluta khor marim* (I never believed it because there is no unity among us. Today we are convinced with each other tomorrow we may take a backseat). These days children do not get to know their history, how come they will know about the future *(manuhe nixor otit naxanile bhobishyot kenekoi xanibo?)*. All they know is to watch television. There are no emotions left in them."

She added further, "As a family we have suffered a lot, our youngest son could not complete his graduation. Throughout his academic life he had to stay in someone else's place and appear for his examinations. Till 2004 there was a psychological torture from the police and administration (they blamed we had a relation with ULFA, where as our son died in March, 1991). *"Manuhe buxi napai ahukhiya pitri aro asohay sontanor bejar"* (people do not understand the trauma of an ailing father and helpless child's grief)."

Ms. Meera Pathak (61 years) is the mother of late Subhasis Pathak alias Ranjan Sarmah, who was killed in an encounter with the army. He was twenty seven years old at the time of his death with a bullet to the forehead. During the encounter, Subhasis was carrying around ninety lakh rupees with him according to another ULFA cadre who was accompanying him at that time. In the beginning, the family thought of going to the court as the death of Subhasis occurred under mysterious circumstances and the wound on his forehead was from a point blank range. But they were advised by the well-wishers not to do so as it would get them no justice.

To talk about Subhasis was painful for Ms. Pathak. In between, she broke down and at times remained silent. The pain was so much that she found it difficult to remember things. She said, Subhasis had left the house at the age of sixteen, soon after his class X examination. This happened when she was away in Vellor, South India for the treatment of her husband who at that time was suspected with oral cancer. She reminisced that Subhasis might have left because someone brainwashed him. Or else his other two brothers would also have joined the outfit. She felt that due to her engagement in his father's ailment a gap between her and her children grew up. Subhasis never came home except once when he was caught in Dibrugarh. By that time the family got used to the fact that they had only two sons (there were three brothers). When he came home, he only stayed for three months and left to never come back again.

Meera Pathak said that she was proud of her son who had a hero's death; *"Xe hat dangi mora nai, Xe xuxi morise beeror dore."*

Ms. Pathak's youngest son Debashis who was also present during the interview said that as long as we would have the fundamental problems in the state we would have ULFA with us. He felt that the government had taken a 'divide and rule policy', therefore the path to a *'Swadhin Asom'* became more difficult. "ULFA needs to rethink their policies and methods to attain a *'Swadhin Asom'*.

Mr. Lohit Ch. Das (82 years) is one of the prominent leaders of the 'Revolutionary Communist Party of India' (RCPI) from Nalbari. He leads a quiet life with his family in one of the corners of Nalbari town. Regarding the ULFA problem, he said that he was not surprised as many cadres were from Nalbari district as it had a history of an armed struggle. He said that ULFA was the offshoot of AASU, which took up arms to address the issues concerning the state. But they went towards Bangladesh and Pakistan for help rather then going to China or Vietnam. He felt at times that everyone needed a group like ULFA to bring certain basic problems of the people to the notice of the government.

He said that Nalbari district had the highest number of unorganized and marginalized labor and this was one of main reasons of a high number of recruitments of boys in the outfit. He said he did not believe in the concept of a *'Swadhin Asom'*. It was just a slogan of ULFA to get attention from the government. At the same time, the government of India had not been taking proper measures to solve this problem. He said there were two groups in the government where one does not want to solve this problem. The reason behind this was that there was a lot of money involved in it. This group in the government was minting money out of the whole insurgency issue.

He said, "The government of India could have solved the problem through Mamoni Raisom Goswami. It would have been a good way of taking help of someone who is apolitical but we have lost the opportunity. Nevertheless, the government should again go for the talks without thinking much of their ego. Otherwise Assam would be another Bangladesh."

When I went to meet **Mr. Ranjit Barman** (37 years) first in the morning to his residence, he was not available then. I had to come back again in the evening and we had a long chat about the conflict situation in the state.

Ranjit Barman is an active member of AGP as the secretary, of the Central Committee. This is one of the prominent regional political parties of the state. They are mainly involved with various political demands like development of the northeastern region, and dual citizenship.

Regarding the law and order situation in the state he said that he did not feel there was any such of a problem.

While speaking on the concept of a *'Swadhin Asom'* he said, "There is no one who will not like the concept of 'Sovereignty' or 'Freedom'. We want a state, which can run itself without the help of anyone. Economic independence is very important and this deprivation has lead to the concept of the *'Swadhin Asom'*. If I am not mistaken recently when there were some irregularities regarding the recruitments of some constables, people sported banners saying *"Paresh Baruah amak bosauk"* (Paresh Baruah save us)! Some people do look at these boys for justice. But at the personal level, I do not support this concept as I do not believe in violence." At the same time, he added, "I see changes in terms of mainland people becoming aware of our existence which was missing earlier. They never have given any value to our lives, but now they recognize our power."

He said. "The future of Assam looks very bleak to me. The human resource is suffering due to this internal conflict in the state. Industrialists do not want to invest here and the education of the children is also getting hampered."

He felt that there was no more popular mass support left for ULFA because of the measures taken by the government. However, he added, "If you look back, our history says that we had hardly a lot of blood shed or wars in this region. The current conflict is the creation of the democratic exploitation. There is no industrialization, economic development and the government has never tried to find out as why ULFA had come into being. ULFA is going strong despite all counter-insurgency. It is because the government is keeping it alive by not addressing the core problems of the state."

Regarding the role of ULFA and the government in the prevailing situation, he said, "ULFA needs to stop all the violence against individuals and the state. Then both the government and ULFA need to come forward for a peaceful discussion."

He added further that the government should remove the 'Armed Forces Special Power Act' as soon as possible.

Dr. Aparajita Saikia (49 years)[2] is a lecturer in one of the prominent colleges in Nalbari. While talking to me Dr. Saikia revealed how disgusted she was with the ULFA problem in the state. She said that she had been living in a place where there was the constant fear of ULFA. The excerpts from the interview are as follows. Besides teaching, she is involved with literary activities.

She said, "There is an unrest in the state; we are scared all the time that anything can happen to us or our beloved ones."

She felt that the whole concept of a *'Swadhin Asom'* would be not feasible at all. She said, "I do not believe in the concept. I do not believe it because to attain it one needs planning and proper guidance, the two things missing on the part of the ULFA leaders. Killing innocent people is not going to bring a *'Swadhin Asom'* to anyhow. Even with a *'Swadhin Asom'* the present leaders will guide Assam to an abysmal darkness as they lack the reign of values to steer it."

She added, "The future of Assam depends upon the next generation. All the bright youngsters have gone out for higher studies and never come back as there is no future in the state. Those who are staying back, either are not hard working or do not have the means. At present, nobody wants to become a good teacher. What would be the future of the budding ones? Recently I have seen many changes in terms of our life style. It has changed dramatically. We have become so mechanized and materialistic that no room is left for the human emotions like love, affections, and respect. In the process we are even losing our beautiful environment."

Regarding the popular mass support towards ULFA, she said that she did not think ULFA was going strong anymore and there was any popular mass support left. In support of them, whatever favor they were getting was because of the fear of the gun. Nobody would like to take a chance with them. "I have seen violence from a close quarter and it destroys everything. I fear for it."

Looking at the on going situation, she felt that ULFA and the government needed to come for a talk. She added, at times the 'Arms Forces Special Power Act' had been stopping *'Arajokota'* (chaos) in the state to an extent.

IV

Ms. Junu Bora (44 years) is the Editor of *'Jonaki Baat'* one of the oldest women's magazine in the state and she is the member of the *'Saudo Asom Pragatisil Nari Santha'*. Regarding the law and order situation in the state, she said, "One of the major problems of Assam is the current law and order situation. The ongoing incidents are the examples of it. There is no human security. There are no political initiatives to tackle the terrorism on the government's part. In the name of law and order, the government is harassing the common people."

While sharing her view on the concept of a *'Swadhin Asom'* she said, "The concept is not acceptable. Without analyzing the statistics of the people supporting it, no one can say that it is the demand of the people of Assam. Majority of our people do not support it. Personally, I also do not support this concept. First, it is not a practical one; secondly, for last thirty years, ULFA could not get the support of the people of Assam on this and thirdly, with a sovereign country our basic problem will not vanish. Rather than asking for a sovereign state, one needs to work out to solve the basic problems of the state and join hand with other movements happening throughout the country."

She felt that ULFA was not going strong due to the counter interagency measures of the government and due to the ceasefire announcement by the 28th battalion's two companies. There was a clear picture of division in the group. She further said that there was no popular mass support for ULFA. ULFA's involvements with extortions, kidnappings, killings, and bombings have made the people of Assam withdrew their support for them. They had failed miserably. The government had taken this problem as a law and order problem rather than a political problem.

Speaking about the role of ULFA and the government, she said, "Both the parties need to sit for an unconditional talk. Both need to leave their egos and escapists mentality and try to bring back peace to the state. They need to have a direct talk with each other without any third party intervention."

She said, the 'Arms Forces Special Power Act' should be withdrawn, as with the help of this act, army was getting atrocious. She said, "They are harassing the common people, raping our women and killing many innocent ones. There is a movement going on, Manipur is asking for removal of this act. In Assam also, people are demanding to remove it. For a democratic atmosphere there is an urgent need to abolish this act."

Ms. Rupali Konwar (23 years)[3] is a research scholar in an institute. Interviewing her helped me introduce with the other students who I interviewed later. The excerpts from the interviews are as follows.

Regarding the insurgency problem, she felt that it was due to the deprivation, unemployment, and geographical isolation of Assam. She added that there was no law and order problem in the state and the common people were being harassed in the name of security checks.

While talking about her understanding of the concept of a *'Swadhin Asom'*, she said that it meant a sovereign Assam! However, she did not support this concept because there was no proper leadership to achieve this and ULFA themselves were confused as what exactly they would want. She added that the state had its own problems like ethnic conflict and 'demands for autonomy'. So amidst all, a *'Swadhin Asom'* was not feasible.

The future of Assam according to her would depend on, how quickly the government would deal with the existing problems in hand. She felt ULFA was going strong because the government had not attacked their main 'hideout' locations.

She felt that there was no popular mass support for ULFA any more because they have killed many innocent people.

Looking into the prevailing situation, she felt ULFA needed to rethink as what they were doing and it was high time that both ULFA and the government would come forward for a talk.

Regarding the 'Arms Forces Special Power Act', she said, "Yes! I know it is in Manipur but I am not aware of it that it is in Assam also. I would not be able to say much about it but I think a few modifications are needed to its current form."

Ms. Pramila Hazarika (23 years)[4] is a postgraduate student of Political Science. Regarding the insurgency problem in the state, she said, "It is due to the unemployment, deprivation, and a feeling of sheer frustration among the people in the society."

Regarding the concept of a *'Swadhin Asom'*, she said, "A greater autonomy can be given to the people of Assam but not a sovereign state. If the entire northeastern states come together then we can think of seceding from India. I can see combined strength and development in that process". Further, she added, "Personally I do not support the concept because ULFA never tried to understand what the people of Assam want. They never uttered a single word on the real issues like illegal immigration. They never showed that they belonged to the masses. They are now involved with terrorist activities and they have taken refugee in a foreign country."

She felt that it was important to take initiatives to solve the prevailing problems of the state. There was a gross violation of human rights going on in the state and that needed prime attention.

She felt that ULFA was going strong due to the loopholes in the counter insurgency system and the lack of consciousness among the common people.

Regarding the popular mass support towards ULFA, she said, "No! At present they do not enjoy the popular mass support as they have moved away from their original issues. In my native place, common people still allow them to take shelter, as they are scared of their guns!"

While speaking on the 'Arms Forces Special Power Act', she said, "It is needed in the state but to avoid misunderstanding we need to have someone who knows the local language to guide the army. There are times when insurgents have killed more people than the army. We need to modify certain sections of the act and subsequently implement it."

Ms. Himani Goswami (26 years)[5] is a postgraduate student in Tourism Management and presently she is getting a fellowship to conduct a research study.

She felt that the various ethnic groups and communities had become aware of their identities of late and people had become greedy for power. Together these have led to the insurgency problem in the state. In addition, the political unrest in the state had made the situation more critical.

Regarding the concept of a *'Swadhin Asom',* she said that it was an impossible concept to achieve. She did not support it because she believed that she had been a citizen of a sovereign country i.e. India.

She added that the future of Assam looked very bleak as there was terror in the society and prompt actions were the need of the hour.

While speaking about ULFA's popular mass support she said, "They do not have that support anymore. In the beginning, the people supported them, as they were our own boys. Now, people do not do so because no one likes to live in fear."

Looking into the prevailing situation, she felt, ULFA needed to engage themselves in development activities to survive as a citizen of this country. Moreover, the government of India should need to bring political stability and good governance that will automatically chase away insurgency problem from the state.

Speaking on the 'Arms Forces Special Power Act', she said, "I am not aware of this particular Act, but from the human rights perspectives I do not support any kind of torture or harassment."

Mr. Dhiren Das (24 years)[6] is a postgraduate student of economics. While talking about the insurgency problem in the state he said, "Due to the insurgency problem, we are having other problems like lack of investment. When it comes to the local and foreign investment, people are scared to invest in a state like Assam."

Speaking on the concept of a *'Swadhin Asom'* he said, "It is not possible to achieve it as the whole region is not developed. How will they manage it? I personally do not believe it. Economically and politically we are very poor to manage it." Regarding the future of Assam, he felt that the government needed to use the natural resources of the state to the fullest.

He said that ULFA had not been vanished completely from the state but it was not that strong anymore. Bangladesh would also remove them from their country. He added further that ULFA did not have the popular mass support. Whatever support they were getting was from the ignorant people for whom they were still the leaders.

Regarding the role of ULFA and government in the on going situation, he felt that both needed to come for a talk to resolve the problem.

He felt that the 'Arms Forces Special Power Act' was very useful to solve the problem of insurgency and a few modifications could be done to make it more people friendly.

Ms. Queen Borah (24 years)[7] is a postgraduate student in Political Science. According to her, the insurgency problem in the state was due to the underdevelopment and unemployment. When asked what was her view on *'Swadhin Asom'*, she said, "It means a sovereign state." She added, "Personally I do not support the concept as with the internal problems like ethnic conflict still very much predominant, it is not feasible to dream of a sovereign country."

The future of Assam did not look bright according to her with so many internal problems in the state.

She felt that ULFA did not enjoy the mass support it used to enjoy earlier. "At present we find many problems within ULFA and their aims have changed too." Earlier it looked that ULFA was still going strong despite the counter-insurgency measures by the government. Gradually it had been fading."

Considering the prevailing situation, she felt that ULFA needed to give up arms and go for a mass support so that in actual terms they could address the basic problems of the state. The government of Assam also needed to address the problems like unemployment, ethnic conflict in the state. To maintain the law and order situation in the state there was a need for the 'Arms Forces Special Power Act'. She said that there was a need for reforms in the act so that there would be no human rights violations.

Mr. Pawan Dutta (26 years)[8] is a postgraduate student in Political Science. While speaking about the insurgency problem in the state he said, "Insurgency is a form of reactions to the government policies. They want to bring a change to the existing situation through insurgency. In Assam's context this problem has increased in the recent past."

The law and order was a problem according to him and he said, "This is because of the insurgency problem in the state and there are loopholes in the army and administrative setup of the state."

Regarding the concept of a *'Swadhin Asom'* he said, "I do not support the concept of a *'Swadhin Asom'*. It is a vague concept, which is not attainable. Constitutionally we should have the status like Jammu & Kashmir as in Assam also we have many ethnic groups and unique problems."

Pawan felt that in the future the identity of the 'Assamese' people would be at stake as the way various groups were getting 'autonomous councils'. The Assamese people would have to fight another battle for their identity.

According to him, ULFA was going strong because the boys in the outfit were working as professionals. That group of boys was neither ideologically motivated nor properly educated. Joining the outfit had become a kind of a job form where they could have an income. This was the main reason why they were still going strong.

He further added that there was no popular mass support left for them as they had been living outside the country.

Looking into the prevailing situation, he felt that both ULFA and the government needed to come forward for a talk without any conditions. Regarding the 'Arms Forces Special Power Act', he said he did not have any idea except that it was there in Manipur.

Before giving the interview, **Mr. Dipankar Kalita** (29 years)[9] wanted to go through the questionnaire and he requested for anonymity. Dipankar is a mechanical engineer by profession. The excerpts of the interview are as follows.

Regarding the insurgency problem in the state he said, "Insurgency is the biggest issue of Assam as of now. Our growth and economic development have taken a back seat. We have been stuck where we were twenty years ago." He said that the law and order was also a problem in the state. People got scared to venture out late at night, as they were not sure about the law and order situation.

Speaking with reference to the concept of a *'Swadhin Asom'* he said, "I do not consider it even as a concept. We are already a free people and we are already in an independent nation. I am an Indian, and I do not consider Assam separate from India. We are an integral part of India. We share the same cultural heritage. Our way of life is same and even our rituals are similar. Our languages have so many similarities. Then why should we think of ourselves as somebody different from India?"

While speaking about the future of Assam he said, "We can rebuild our future. However, we need a few changes in our mindset. We should embrace a work culture instead of the *'Bandh'* culture. Say a firm 'No' to militancy. Let us all think and talk about development not destruction. We need a good leader and that is what we are lacking as of now."

He added further, "ULFA is not going strong and in fact they are going desperate. They should understand that we, the people of Assam want peace, not violence. We had enough of bloodshed, we had our share of woes, and we do not need any more. I would like to request them to come back home. We need them to build Assam not to destroy it." He said,

"ULFA had their share of mass support once, not anymore. Moreover, it is because the people of Assam initially assumed that ULFA is there to fight against the injustice done by corrupt politicians and Government officials. Therefore, people were happy to support them. And ULFA mistook it to be the support for their cause of an independent Assam. But most of the Assamese people never thought themselves to be separate from India. So slowly, their support has shrunken. The problem with ULFA is that they never want even to think on the line common people are thinking. They think that majority still supports them but which is not the case."

Looking into the present situation Dipankar Kalita felt, "ULFA first need to stop treating people who speaks against their ideas to be their enemies. They should stop blaming others and start retrospection. They need to look back and see what they have given to the state. They need to change themselves. We certainly do not want another Bosnia or an Afghanistan". He further said, "The problem with the government is that it never worked for the people although it was formed by the people. If those politicians have done something for the people of the state instead of only thinking about filling their own pockets, we would have seen a different Assam then what we see today. They were always busy feeding themselves and let the nation go to the dogs. I really wish there will be some able leadership someday which will change the face of the nation."

Mr. Durga Prashad Bora (80 years) has held many important posts under the government of Assam. He is also an active member of a club and a non-governmental organization. Presently, he is leading a quite retired life due to health reasons. Excerpts from the interview are as follows.

While speaking on the insurgency problem in the state he said, "Certain thing go against the administration but at the same time what they are doing is also not correct. They are trying to gain something and in return harassing the common people." He further added that the law and order problem has become a common problem of the region. The region is not only faced by ULFA, but other ethnic problems too are gradually becoming stronger.

He said that the concept of a *'Swadhin Asom'* is totally a vague concept. The state cannot declare a region sovereign. "What will happen to the common people? I personally do not support this concept because first of all we do not have resources with which we can survive as a nation. Secondly, India is a huge country and I am proud to be part of it. Thirdly, the present political situation is disturbed because their ideology is completely vague."

Durga Prashad Bora felt that the future of Assam depended on the political situation of the state. He said, "If the extremist elements could be eliminated, Assam is sure to progress in the near future. Progress is not possible in the present situation."

He felt that the government's counter-insurgency measures were not successful since ULFA had got their base in Bangladesh. At the same time, he felt that there was no mass support left for ULFA. Its ideology was never clear.

Looking in to the prevailing situation, he felt "ULFA should stop killing the innocent people. With their destructive attitude, they are neither going to gain anything nor can provide anything to others. They should stop this attitude first." Adding to this he said, "It is not easy to completely put an end to this problem. The government tries to bring some development but because of these elements it has to step back."

Regarding the 'Armed Forces Special Power Act', he said, "I can not say it is not important. Looking at the present situation, I feel that it is required. ULFA is also paving the way for smaller insurgent groups to grow, I think it is required."

Mr. Ravindra Ramchiyari (48 years) is a regular reader of newspapers. In fact, he loves to read old newspapers at times. He runs a small business, which is hardly enough to sustain him and his spouse. At present, they are partially dependent on their daughter. Before talking to me, he wanted to know the questions before and he came prepared next day. We had a long discussion revolving the interview. The excerpts of the interview are given below.

He felt that there was a law and order problem in the state. "The common people are feeling insecure. The reasons behind this insecurity are unemployment, illegal immigration leading to population explosion, exploitation by the government and corruption in the administration. The dropout boys are being used by a group of people."

While speaking about the concept of a *'Swadhin Asom'*, he said "*ULFA r Swadhin Asom or bisoye bhabiboloi kunu adhar puwa nai* (there is no base to think about ULFA's sovereign Assam)." We are already the citizens of a sovereign state, therefore, I do not believe in it. If we talk of a *'Swadhin Asom'*, there will be more demands of other groups becoming sovereign."

He said that if anyone wanted to curb the problem of ULFA, one had to address the basic issues like unemployment, illegal immigration, corruption and the quality of education among the youth. Army operations were not the answers to this problem.

Regarding the mass support towards ULFA, he had to say, "People do not love them like before, as in the name of freedom, ULFA has been involved with a lot of subversive activities. Many boys in the name of a *'Swadhin Asom'* are now leading a very luxurious life and if required they are killing their own comrades."

Reflecting in to the on going situation, he said, "ULFA needs to come back and work with the common people for humanity rather than sovereignty. The government of India should have the responsibility of bringing back these boys to the mainstream. We are citizens of a sovereign democratic country. We are having an elected government and constitution through which we need to address all these grievances in a democratic way. At this moment, we are lacking humanity and self-actualization. We need them for a better future."

Adding to this he said, "The 'Armed Forces Special Power Act' is undemocratic act which violates our human rights."

When I asked **Nirupama Borgohain,** a noted novelist, columnist and 'Sahitya Academy' award winner about the situation in the state, she said, "During the 'Assam Movement', the whole concept of violence grew. Along with it grew terrorism and secessionism. As we are situated on the periphery, this group had an advantage and they flourished with the help of outsiders." Due to the unemployment in the state, this problem grew even more and it had certain pockets like Kakopathar and Nalbari where it had its base. In places like Kakopathar, a section of the population was warriors by nature, and in Nalbari, people were stricken with poverty.

Regarding the concept of a *'Swadhin Asom'* she said, "*Olik Sowapon dekhise* (they are dreaming an impossible dream). The Indian Army is an unequal force to fight with. Until now, many violent wars have been fought but no one has been successful in front of the Indian Army. During the Assam Movement, many intellectuals have given their support to the cause, but with ULFA, a very few people had this support. In the interior villages, they have a support, but again many people have supported them out of fear. Many ethnic groups of Assam are yet to support ULFA, for instance the people in the 'Barak Valley' have no support for them. Now moneymaking is the main objective of this organization. Very few boys have gone with an ideology who are no longer alive." Adding further, she said that the government of India had also become strict in its objectives. It was time that ULFA rethink for themselves.

While talking about the civil society in Assam, she said, "Assamese people by nature are callous. They are self-centered, not bothered beyond their own property and family. The middle class in general is not at all concerned with the problems of the society unless they themselves fall victim to it. There were a few handfuls of people who spoke, wrote and held discussions extensively against ULFA but beyond that no one has taken any steps."

Speaking on the on going situation of the state, **Indibor Dewri** a well-known writer who has extensively written on the issues of ethnic groups in the state said, "The lack of attention towards this area since British period is the main reason of the armed conflicts in the state."

He added further, "In 1912 Ghanashyam Baruah said that we are being deprived of our dues compared to other states of the country. The tea industry was there but it was a colonial enclave. In fact, after India became independent the same process followed. The land of the 'Moran- Mataks' were taken away by the tea industry and the workers were also brought from outside. Along the *Marwaris* followed. The feeling of deprivation and alienation grew which led to the armed conflict. The people of Assam are divided in to different sections. The upper caste Assamese have been hegemonic so far and there is a feeling of alienation among the other castes and ethnic groups. This armed struggle will not be a successful one. However, if possible we need to try and use our resources within the state itself rather then allowing them to be taken outside."

Regarding the civil society in the state he said, "The civil society in Assam is not united (*Asomor Nagorik Samaj akgot nohoi*). There is vested interest among the civil society and the hegemonic attitude still prevails. Personally I do not have much faith in this civil society as there is elitist attitude and this will not help in bringing the people of Assam together." Adding to this he said, "There is no government's will to tackle the problem of ULFA. Even in our society the attitude of the people is soft, where they mention "ULFA" as 'boys gone out',as if these boys have not grown up and not responsible for their actions! These boys have spoken on some basic issues of the state and therefore they got support in one point of time. Now the scene has changed and the attitude government has taken is repressive. Unless and until these basic issues are addressed we will keep facing these type of conflict in the state."

Padmashree **Birendra Nath Dutta,** former President of Assam Sahitya Sabha, speaking on the emergence of ULFA said, "It was spearheaded by *'Chatra Santha'* (Students Union) during the Assam Movement. The Assam Movement was an anti-foreigners movement and these boys also had the same agenda. They got the support of the Assamese people as they spoke on behalf of them. People did not like Hiteshwar Saikia and there was this 'Robinhood' image being created for this group."

He said, "I do not understand their concept of a *'Swadhin Asom'*. Until now, they have not been able to convince us as for who will be in the *'Swadhin Asom'*. When, *Mahapurush Shankardeva* spoke of *'Asom'* he meant the 'Ahom' population. Can they think of an Assam without the contribution of *Shankardeva* and *Jyotiprashad Agarwala?* In fact, *Shankardeva* has extensively praised India. What will be the composition of their *'Swadhin Asom'*? The political India was always changing and British made it one for their administrative purpose. Culturally and spiritually, we share so much with rest of India. Our Assamese language had come from 'Sanskrit'. I keep wondering how ULFA is going to rule us in a *'Swadhin Asom'*. Will there be a democratic state or a dictatorship? How are they going to separate us from the cultural and spiritual India?"

The support ULFA was getting was due to the fear among the people according to Shri Dutta. Adding to this he said, "In the upper Assam area the support base is due to the ethnic composition and in the lower Assam there was a history of armed struggle and poverty. They wanted to get rid of the Bangladeshis! Where are they now? The lower rank cadres are struggling here and the leaders are away in Bangladesh living a safe life. In addition, they are in wanton killings, who will support all these? So I do not think there is a mass support anymore."

While speaking on the civil society in Assam he said, "The civil society in Assam is very fragmented. Now we can hope it will play a cementing role where there is a space for them. But when it comes to the ULFA problem, I feel that the role of the civil society has been playing very minimal. Many have tried to intervene but nothing has come out so far. It is the government of India's issue and it has international ramification. Regarding Sahitya Sabha's role in this issue he said, "One should not mingle political issue and literature. The Sahitya Sabha should solely concentrate on the literary activities and the ULFA problem is a political problem."

Noted social activist and Megsasay Award winner **Sandip Pandey** felt that the prevailing situation was a political problem and it had its roots due to aspirations not being fulfilled and to an extent of identity politics. He said, "The political crisis has turned into a violent situation and the role government of India has played is equally violent. Violence is not the answer to the aspirations of the people. The government needs to give a democratic solution to the problems arising in a state. Here, the situation is due to unemployment. The government has to distinguish between a crime and an insurgency situation, both deserving a separate handling."

Speaking about the role of the civil society he said, "Civil society's role is very important here as the government is behaving like a guard. The civil society has to convince the government that grievances must be addressed and those who have taken a wrong path must be brought back to the political mainstream." Pointing out at Kashmir he said, "Look at the Kashmir election, where people have turned out for exercising their political right though there was a call to boycott the election. And this has happened due to the role government of India and Pakistan have played for the last four years. 'Dialogue' is very important in any situation than repressive measures. It is the most civilized way of achieving peace and harmony. The 'Armed Forces Special Power Act' and similar acts are not the answers to address a conflict situation."

Well-known economist and academician **Prof. Dilip Baruah** felt that the concept of '*Swadhin Asom*' or demand for it was unrealistic. The whole issue came when the state was underdeveloped and the central government neglected the northeast region. However, the situation has changed now. The government of India has taken right steps to open up new avenues and departments for this region. In fact, the centre has given enough money to the state but most of the times the grant is going back due to lack of schemes to utilize it. According to Montek Singh Ahluwalia the centre gave us ten thousand croers during the 10th plan and the state government of Assam used four thousand four hundred croers only, the rest went back. It is not that we are getting step motherly attitude. We failed to utilize the money allocated to us.

He said that the government of India had failed to tackle the problems at the nascent. The Assamese people had to fight every time for every needs of its. "Look at Andhra Pradesh! The same situation prevails. It is only when peaceful demands turn into a violent form, the government of India takes a note. Now they are wasting croers of money every year in the name of law and order. The state government is not using the money for the development. There is a lack of efficient administrator, use of resources and they are not keeping in view the production in the state. Production is important than the fiscal gain of a state."

While talking about the civil society in Assam Prof. Baruah said, "The civil society in Assam has become conscious but this consciousness needs to spread out to the interior places. Against illegal migration, people have come together. For the conflict situation, they need to come forward soon.

May be somewhere we have failed to make the civil society understand the situation. We need to work above our personal interests and pave the way for those who have been working for the society. Acknowledging the contribution of others will help us be a stronger civil society. Today's youth need to concentrate in these aspects, they should not follow their elders blindly, and they need a different perspective. Here, the media also has an important role to play. They need to give coverage to the civil society initiatives and dialogues for a better future.

Looking into the prevailing situation, he felt that both the government and ULFA needed to have a talk without any conditions.

NOTES

1. name changed for maintaining confidentiality.
2. name changed for maintaining confidentiality.
3. name changed for maintaining confidentiality.
4. name changed for maintaining confidentiality.
5. name changed for maintaining confidentiality.
6. name changed for maintaining confidentiality.
7. name changed for maintaining confidentiality.
8. name changed for maintaining confidentiality.
9. name changed for maintaining confidentiality.

Ms. Parul Sarma

Mr. Surendranath Dahotia

Mr. Brahma Dutta Mahanta and Ms. Thuluki Mahanta

Mr. Gaurikanta Gohain and Barnali Gohain

Shri Chakreshwar Mahanta
(Satradhikar of Shri Mayamora Hatigarh Mulani Satra)

Dr. J.K. Mahanta

Mr. Jatindra Nath Neog

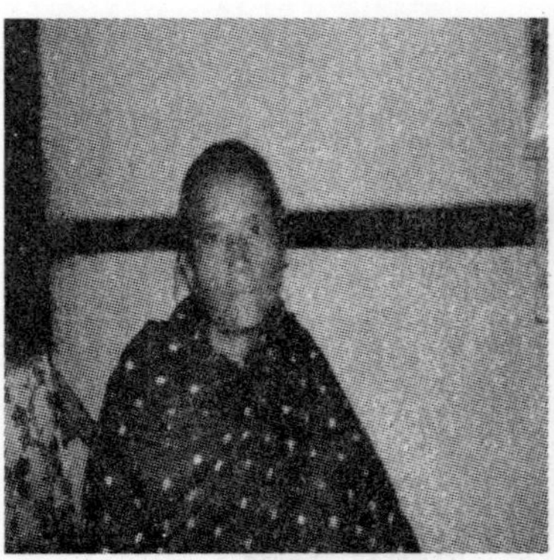

Ms. Jyoti Hazarika

Mr. Kumbheswar Hazarika
alias Billu Saikia

Ms. Gitimoni Gogoi Hazarika with her Mother and Son

Photograph of late Basanta Deka

Mr. Brojen Choudhury

Ms. Nalini Baruah

Late Azad Baruah with a camera

Ms. Meera Pathak

Late Subhasis Pathak in an undisclosed camp of ULFA

Mr. Lohit Ch. Das with his wife

5

Response and Reality

I

Through the study, it was intended to project a picture of ULFA and the civil society's stand to the prevailing situation in the state of Assam. The interactions with the civil society representatives of Tinsukia, Dibrugarh, Nalbari, and Guwahati brought to notice that everyone was tired of the violence, which have continued for the last three decades. All of them have expressed a desire that the government of India and ULFA would need to come for a genuine talk and find a peaceful solution to this problem.

The study was formulated on three hypotheses. The first one was that ULFA had enjoyed the mass popular support in the initial years of its formation with the people generally heeding to its diktats in terms of boycott calls and the like, whether out of fear or for their 'Robinhood Image'. The civil society representatives confirmed this assumption by agreeing to. They said that there had been a popular mass support for ULFA in the initial phase as they took the image of 'Robinhood' by punishing the corrupt officials, illegal business men and the illicit liquor sellers. However, there were a few who felt that the mass support for the organization still prevailed. Initially this support was reinforced with the belief that whatever ULFA had been doing, was for the betterment of the Assamese society. But, the organization had turned out to be a terrorist outfit who did not mind bombing and killing the commoners.

In the initial phase ULFA along with AASU, AJYCP and AGP spoke against the illegal immigration. However, ULFA's stand on this had been replaced by their change in attitude towards the immigrants. In one of their *'Prachar Patra'*, they said how much the East Bengal immigrants had contributed to the agriculture and economy of the state.[1] The civil society also expressed that initially ULFA's stand was against foreigners (especially East Bengal immigrants). Of late, this belief was shrouded by their action of taking shelter in Bangladesh itself.

The civil society also detested ULFA's bomb blasts at various points of time. They expressed that ULFA was targeting the common people who had been living hand to mouth. Some of the respondents were criticizing ULFA, as they were not paying attention to the problem of other ethnic groups other than the mainstream Assamese population. In fact, the respondents expressed that ULFA's complete U-turn in terms of their earlier vision lead the state into a grave situation.

The civil society representatives expressed that ULFA was going strong despite counter-interagency measures due to one good reason. A low intensity conflict has many stakeholders. It is like an industry. Some of the respondents have confirmed that the counter-insurgency measures, the state was initiating had not been successful as the state (represented by the security forces) had also been a stakeholder of the conflict industry. The creation of SULFA was a short-term solution crafted by the government. According to one of the police officers, "There were times when, relatives were also made to surrender as ULFA to get the incentives." To stop insurgency by providing money and small arms to the youth involved in terrorist activities by the government was not supported by the respondents.

Moreover, a few said that the loopholes in the security measures were another reason for the failure. The counter-insurgency measures in majority of the cases harassed the common people and a majority felt that the government should abolish the 'Armed Forces (Special Powers) Act' from the state. To a great extent, the support for ULFA was continuing due to the scares left by the '*Rhino*' and the '*Bajrang*' operations and a numerous army atrocities on women, youth, and innocent villagers in the name of counter-insurgency. Many women were raped during those operations. Spontaneously women's organizations were formed in protest against the atrocities.[2] A few of the respondents felt that there was a need for this act. Otherwise, there would be a threat from the insurgents, who would make the lives of the common people miserable. The civil society respondents had a mix reaction towards the act. A section said that there was an immediate need to remove the act. According to them, it was one of the repressive and undemocratic ways of handling the situation in the state. However, a section felt that this act was needed to overcome a fear brought forth by the militants. They said that they had experienced and seen what happened in the villages in the name of giving shelter to those boys. The extortion demands and threatening were some of the means used by the militants and they created a fear psychosis and pressure among the common people. In addition, there were instances of people being killed to fulfill one's personal scores. Therefore, many felt that the act had been shielding them from ULFA.

One of the objectives of ULFA was to liberate Assam, (a land of about seventy nine thousand square Km) through armed national liberation struggle from the clutches of the illegal occupation of India and to establish a sovereign independent Assam.[3] This had been the first objectives of ULFA and for the last thirty years, they had been carrying out the armed struggle to attain it. While expressing their views on ULFA, its ideology and objectives, the representatives said that majority did not support the '*Swadhin Asom*' concept. This can be seen from the following pie chart.

A total eighty seven per cent respondents said that they did not support the concept '*Swadhin Asom*' and thirteen per

Figure : Support for "*Swadhin Asom*"

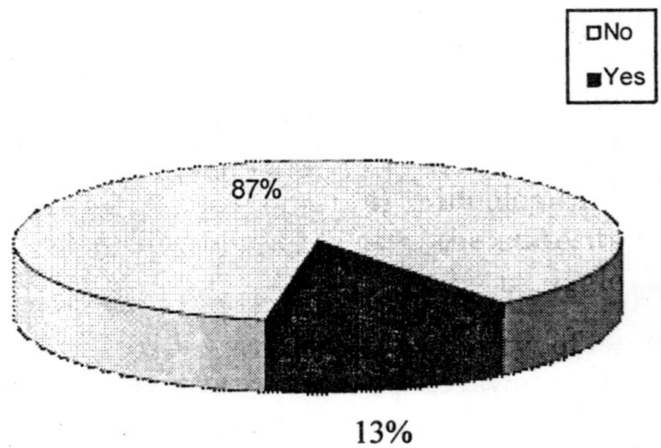

cent said that they supported the concept. However, there were representatives who felt that a 'Greater Autonomy' could be given to the people of Assam.

The second hypothesis of the study was that the support level of ULFA had declined over the years, in the face of an unprecedented surge in terrorist activities on its part, coupled by the fact that the outfit was then widely believed to be under the influence of external forces (cross-border linkages of actors). Majority respondent said that ULFA had turned out to be a terrorist organization and they had been under the influence of Bangladeshi elements. Many expressed that ULFA was going strong due to the help from the foreign countries. One respondent said that the Chinese ammunitions found with the group also pointed its linkage with that nation apart from Bangladesh and Pakistan.

Our third hypothesis of the study was to find out the long running and protracted struggle of ULFA and the question that arises about what actually had been sustaining the ULFA movement. A wide range of plausible factors were:

1) Easy availability of small arms
2) Interests of vested groups driven by stakes in the "business" of terrorism
3) Presence of too many unemployed youths in the State who become easy targets for the outfit's recruitment drives,
4) Ideological concerns among its sympathizers within the state itself, might account for the sustenance of the struggle

Majority of the respondents expressed that it was unemployment and because of the lack of development in the state that were the reason of sustenance of ULFA. The exploitative nature of the centre towards the state is also helping this movement to sustain according to a few.

A section said that the easy money, gun power, and lucrative life style had driven youths to be involved with the terrorist activities. Majority of the respondents felt that there was no ideological influences that motivated these boys any longer. Some shared that there had been a system of payroll for the militants.

None of the respondents felt that the organization was somehow linked with other smaller insurgent groups in the state. There were times the civil society representatives had questioned ULFA's plan as how they would go to deal with the ethnic groups' issues and their demands within the state.

The civil society respondents felt that besides a *'Swadhin Asom'*, other issues raised by ULFA had some logical background. They felt that the government of India needed to give attention to those issues. In northeast, most of the cases, the government of India tried to solve the problems viewing it as a law and order problem. They said that there was no political will when it came to solving the conflict situation in the state. There should have been an urgent need to have a dialogue and discussion between the government of India and ULFA. The long drawn hide and seek attitude on the part of the government and ULFA would not going to bring peace in the state. The dialogue between these two parties should not have any conditions.

The respondents expressed that they no longer considered ULFA as 'our boys' anymore. People realized that 'the boys' had disappointed them. The ULFA had fallen prey to external support who had not been fighting for the cause of the Assamese society. At present, civil society of Assam is doubtful regarding the role of ULFA.

II

A central feature of civil society is the concept of social capital, used first by Jacobs (1961:138), developed by Coleman (1988), and explored empirically by Putnam (1993, 1995b, 1996a,b). Social capital inheres in such human relationships as marriage, associational memberships, and friendships. The density and frequency of these social relations promote trust, adherence to group norms, cooperation, and reciprocity (Coleman, 1988:97-100; Putnam, 1993, 1995a). In these associations, people build relationships of trust and mutual aid. Trust, a key ingredient of civil society, is vital for sustaining the economic well- being as well (Fukuyama, 1995:12; Granovetter, 1985; Putnam et al., 1995). The civil society has always drawn its strength from voluntarism and social capital. Unfortunately, in Assam it is waiting for some one else to tackle the problem of the armed conflict in the state and there is a lack of trust among the civil society itself. The ULFA problem is a political issue where the government and ULFA have to take the initiative for a solution. Here, the civil society also has a vital role to play when it comes to put an end to the violence. Throughout my conversations with the civil society representatives, it was found that every one wanted a peaceful solution of this perennial problem. However, all are waiting for someone else to take the lead. They had tremendous hope on Peoples'

Consultative Group (PCG), which was lead by Mamoni Raisom Goswami. But, the PCG also became impasse and then came the pro- talk ceasefire group of ULFA. The leaders from 'A' and 'C' companies of 28th battalion of ULFA came overground in the month of June 2008. The ceasefire group had established three designated camps in Tinsukia and Nalbari. One camp was closed down in Tinsukia (Sadiya) due to security reasons (like inmates running away from it). There was a tremendous hope that there would be talks between the government of India and ULFA, when the group came forth. The pro-talk group had been demanding a 'Full Autonomy' similar to that of Jammu and Kashmir.[4] The group while addressing the civil society comprising academicians, students, journalists, voluntary workers, and writers in Omeo Kumar Das Institute of Social Change and Development, Guwahati in July 2008 said, "Our duty is to build up a favorable environment and public opinion for a talk between the government and central committee of ULFA. From Sadiya to Dhuburi we will build up public opinion for the talk. We will be the catalyst between the government of India and ULFA."[5] During a personal interview, Mrinal Hazarika one of the leaders of pro-talk group again repeated the same to me. Of late, this group was saying that they would be going back to the jungle if the government would not take any initiatives in terms of giving a 'Full Autonomy' and an 'Upper House' in the state.[6] The same report said that they were preparing the 'Charter of Demands' which, they would be presenting to the Prime Minister of India. Until now, the government of India has not commented on the issues demanded by the pro-talk group. The ULFA's central leadership has not commented anything, on the contrary, have expelled all the members of the ceasefire group.

Another characteristic of the civil society in Assam is that it is very fragmented in nature. The responses of the civil society vary in terms of their concern towards the issue. The response of a civil society representative from Guwahati is different from the one from Kakopathar, which could be seen in the narratives. Unlike other movements and issue-based demands made by the civil society in Assam, the issue of ULFA does not draw the attention to them the way it should have. Many a times the civil society is indifferent towards the violence. According to Pradip Phanjoubam a noted Journalist and Editor of *Imphal Free Press*,

> "The civil society in the entire northeast is badly fractured and may not be quite what the term is generally understood to mean. The term civil society itself presupposed certain shared values and qualities regardless of religion and community affiliations. But in the Northeast, these shared values are what have been relegated into the background. Hence, when we talk of students' community or youth or women, there ought not to be any need for prefixing these understandings with community and religion specific qualifications. This however has been far from the truth and therefore there has always been very little prospect to generalize the region's problems. A few examples will illustrate. When we talk of the needs of students or youth or women communities, the nomenclatures themselves ought to have been self-explanatory of the nature of the problems. The reality however is otherwise in the northeast, where every ethnic community forms its own students, youth, women organizations, etc., each with very different and more often than not sectarian agendas to pursue. Often again these pursuits of the different "civil societies" work at cross purposes, accentuating, rather than solving problems."[7]

Violence has become a part of the lives of the people in the states. Once there is a blast or encounter killing usually, there is a spontaneous *'bandh'*. Then people pick up the pieces and move on with their lives, they have become immune to it. Lack of development has been cited by the civil society representatives as one of the reasons of armed conflict in the region. Recently the state government asked for forty five thousand crore rupees from the 13th Finance Commission to revive the insurgency hit economy. The list heads by about nine thousand crore rupees only for 'Police Modernization'. The state's main losses are due to infrastructure damage, flight of business and maintenance of a huge paramilitary force among others.[8]

The people in Assam are exposed to both state and militant violence in a regular interval. This insensitive nature towards violence is indeed a dangerous indication for a democracy where the civil society plays a significant role. So far the Indian state has been firm in addressing the conflicts and in such a backdrop, the civil society has to make avail the space given to them. Now the militant groups are encroaching upon this space. There is an urgent need to use the space of civil society for actualizing the true democratic rights of the citizens. Assam had a heritage of *'Raij Mel'* where all the villagers came together for a purpose. There is a need for reviving the concept for a better future. Here the *'Panchayati Raj Institution (PRI)'* can play a crucial role. The *'Gram Sabha'* concept has very much been derived from the *'Raij Mel'*. Through *PRI* or Local Self Governance, representatives are elected directly by the people, who on behalf of them carry out the governance matters at the grass-root level. Gram Panchayat is the first step towards a participatory bottom up development. It helps the development to take place from the local level to the national level.[9]

The civil society can make avail of the space given to them through *'Gram Sabha'* to ascertain their democratic rights. For an accountable government, sustainable development, and durable peace, *'Gram Sabha'* will be an excellent forum for civil society to make use.

The Telegraph reports that the pro-talks group of the ULFA has sought an urgent discussion with the Assam government as their cadres were getting frustrated after waiting for more than a year. "If we do not get a positive response, we will have to decide on our future course of action," Prabal Neog, a leader of the pro-talks faction, who has been camping in the capital Guwahati since August 19, told. He said he would meet the Principal Secretary (Home) S.C. Das as soon as he returns from Delhi. Neog said the cadres were frustrated and it had become difficult for the leaders to keep on convincing them that there would be some progress. Several cadres had already deserted the designated camps in that past few months and a few had rejoined ULFA while some surrendered to the security forces. Jiten Dutta, another leader of the group, said the blame would rest entirely on the government if talks would fail that time and the cadres would take some drastic steps. "We will not say now what we will do but we will take some decisive steps. The government has turned a deaf ear towards the issue. Despite repeated requests to clear its stand, there is simply no response from the government. This will be our final meeting with the government as we want to clear the air once and for all," he warned. The cadres of the pro-talks group are at present housed in three designated camps in the Tinsukia and Nalbari Districts.[10]

REFERENCES

1. Referred in Mahanta, Nani, 2005, *Terrorism in Assam: The Case of ULFA,* Unpublished Doctoral Thesis, Department of Political Science, GauhatiUniversity, Guwahati, p. 86

2. Referred in First Chapter

3. www.geocities.com/CapitolHill

4. 'ULFA doves use SMS to spread Peace' *The Times of India,* Thursday, January 8, 2009

5. Translated from the original transcript in Assamese by the author

6. 'Dabi Mani Nolole Habiloi Ghuri Xabo Alochona Panthi' *Dainik Janambhumi,* Wednesday, February 11, 2009

7. Kamala Saikia Memorial Trust Lecture, "Reassessing our Wars: A Northeast Journalist Perspective, 09.08. 2004

8. 'Cry for Damage- Repair Funds' *The Telegraph*, Friday, December 19 , 2008

9. Barman, Prateeti, 2005, *Local Self-Governance, Civil Society and Peace Prospect: A Case Study of Nalbari District*, Assam, Unpublished Project Report, OKDISCD, Guwahati, p. 15.

10. *The Telegraph*, 20.08.2009.

Postscript

Three major explosions rocked Assam's principal city Guwahati's Birubari, Bhangagarh and Bhootnath localities on the first day of 2009, leaving 5 persons dead and more than 50 injured. However, it ended with the arrest of the ULFA's chairman, Arabinda Rajkhowa, and the deputy commander-in-chief' Raju Baruah in Dhaka, Bangladesh. The rebel leader's wife and two children were also among those handed over to Indian authorities. Before, Bangladesh's security agencies had arrested ULFA's foreign secretary Sashadhar Choudhury and the finance secretary Chitraban Hazarika from a house in Dhaka's up-market locality on November 1, 2009. The government of India has been blaming that Bangladesh has been a safe haven for the insurgent outfits and categorically they have dismissed it. Of late, the change in the political scenario in Bangladesh has brought out this result. Prime Minister Sheikh Hasina has also initiated several measures to address the institutional deficits in the security machinery, including the formation of a seventeen member National Committee on 'Militancy Resistance and Prevention', and has created a South Asian Anti-Terrorism Task Force to curb cross-border terrorism.

Presently, all the prominent leaders of ULFA are now in Indian custody except the commander-in-chief Paresh Baruah. Soon after the arrest of Sashadhar Choudhury and Chitraban Hazarika, People's Committee for Peace Initiatives in Assam (PCPIA), an umbrella body of twenty-eight different organizations of the State headed by Lachit Bordoloi (member of PCG) called upon the government of India to initiate the process of talk with ULFA. It remains to be seen if the government will display the wisdom to consolidate these advantages. Looking into the present situation it seems that the government of India has been successful in capturing the leaders of ULFA, but it will be interesting to see how far it will be able to bring durable peace to the region, as there are many stakeholders in the political economy of insurgency. The number of people gathered to have a glimpse of the leaders and the welcome they showered towards them again raised questions like 'is there very much a soft corner for the boys?'

Bibliography

Books

Barman, Prateeti, 2005, *Local Self-Governance, Civil Society, and Peace Prospect: A Case Study of Nalbari District, Assam*, OKDISCD, Guwahati, (Unpublished Project Report)

Baruah, Sanjib (ed.), 2009, *Beyond Counter-Insurgency: Breaking the Impasse in Northeast India*, Oxford University Press, New Delhi

Baruah, Sanjib, 2007, *Postfrontier Blues: Toward a New Policy Framework for Northeast India*, Policy Studies 33, East-West Center Washington

Bharali, Udayaditya, 1996, *Parag Kumar Dasar Nirbachita Rachanawali*, Udangshree Publications, Guwahati

Bhuyan, Abhijit, 2006, *Gandhian Non-Violence as a Means of Dispute Settlement in Assam: A Case Study of Tamulpur Anchalik Gramdan Sangh, Kumarikata*, Peace Studies, OKDISCD, Guwahati

Chadha, Vivek, 2005, *Low Intensity Conflicts in India: An Analysis*, Sage Publications, New Delhi

Chakra Behut Dhali Paril Abhimanyu, *A Collection of articles on Parag Kumar Das*, 1997, Udangshree Publications, Guwahati

Chandoke, Neera, 2003, *The Conceits of Civil Society*, Oxford University Press, New Delhi

Das, Samir Kumar, 1994, *ULFA: A Political Analysis*, Ajanta Publications, New Delhi

Das, Samir Kumar, 2007, *Conflict and Peace in India's Northeast: The Role of Civil Society*, Policy Studies 42, East-West Center, Washington

Dutta, Anuradha, Bhuyan, Ratna (ed.), 2007, *Genesis of Conflict and Peace*, Akansha Publishing House, New Delhi

Elliott, Carolyn M., 2003, *Civil Society and Democracy: A Reader*, Oxford University Press, New Delhi

Gokhale, Nitin, 1998, *The Hot Brew: The Assam Tea Industry's Most Turbulent Decade (1987-1997)*, Spectrum Publications, Guwahati

Goswami, Triveni, 2006, *Role of Women as Peace Builders with Special Reference to Nagaland*, Peace Studies, OKDISCD, Guwahati

Hussain, Imdad (ed.), 2005, *The Guwahati Declaration and the Road to Peace*, Akansha Publishing House, New Delhi

Hussain, Wasbir, 2006, *Homemakers without the Men: Assam's Widows of Violence*, Indialog Publications Pvt. Ltd., New Delhi

Jayaram, N., (ed.), 2005, *On Civil Society—Issues and Perspectives*, Sage Publications, New Delhi

Kaviraj, Sudipta, Khilnani, Sunil (ed.), 2001, *Civil Society: History and Possibilities*, Cambridge University Press, New Delhi

Kh. Devi, Elizabeth, 2006, *A Study on the Social Background of Insurgents in Assam with Special Reference to ULFA*, Peace Studies, OKDISCD, Guwahati, (Unpublished Project Report)

Mahanta, Nani, 2005, *Terrorism in Assam: The Case of ULFA*, Department of Political Science, Gauhati University, Guwahati, (Unpublished Doctoral Thesis)

Misra, Udayon, 2000, *The Periphery Strikes Back: Challenges to the Nation-State in Assam and Nagaland,* Indian Institute of Advanced Study, Shimla

Nag, Sajal, 2002, *Contesting Marginality: Ethnicity, Insurgency and Subnationalism in North-East India,* Manohar Publishers & Distributors, New Delhi

Pandey, B.B. 1997, *Gender Triumphs Unarmed in the Hostile Gorges: Re-Discovery of Border Tagins,* Directorate of Research Government of Arunachal Pradesh, Itanagar

Pandey, Nishchal N, 2008, *India's North-Eastern Region: Insurgency, Economic Development and Linkages with South-East Asia,* Manohar Publishers & Distributors, New Delhi

Paragar Kisu Prashna: Kisu Uttar, A Collection of articles of Parag Kumar Das, 1998, Udangshree Publications, Guwahati

Rammohan, E.N, 2005, *Insurgent Frontiers: Essays from the Northeast,* India Research Press, New Delhi

Roy, Ramashray, Miri, Sujata, Goswami, Sndhya (ed.), 2007, *Northeast India: Development, Communalism and Insurgency,* Ashish Publishing House, New Delhi

Saikia, Jaideep (ed.), 2007, *Frontier in Flames: Northeast India in Turmoil,* Penguin Books India Ltd., New Delhi

Sen Geeti, (ed.), 2006, *Where the Sun Rises When Shadows Fall the North-east,* Oxford University Press, New Delhi

Sengupta, Dipankar, Kumar Singh, Sudhir (ed.), 2004, *Insurgency in North-East India: The Role of Bangladesh,* Authorpress Global Network, New Delhi

Tendon, Rajesh, Mohanty, Ranjita (ed.), 2003, *Does Civil Society Matter: Governance in Contemporary India,* Sage Publications, New Delhi

Articles

Beteille, Andre, Citizenship, State and Civil Society

Fearon, James D., Laitin, David D. *Ethnicity, Insurgency, and Civil War.*

Flyvbjerg, Bent, 1998, *Habermas and Foucault: Thinkers for Civil Society?*

Joseph, Sarah, *Society vs. State? Civil Society, Political Society, and Non-Party Political Process in India*

Ross, Marc, Howard, 2001, *Psychocultural Interpretations and Dramas: Identity Dynamics in Ethnic Conflict*

Websites

www.geocities.com/CapitolHill

www.jstor.org

www.satp.org

www.acdis.uiuc.edu/Research/

www.globalpolicy.org/ngos/aid

www.expressindia.com

www.assamtimes.org

www.apfanews.com

www.outlookindia.com

Annexures

ANNEXURE I

Interview Schedule for Youth, Women, Teachers, Social Activists and Local Media Personnel

I.

1. Name: 2. Age:

3. Sex: 4. Occupation:

5. Religion: 6. Caste:

7. Educational qualifications:

8. Date: Time: Location:

II.

1. Are you a member of any student/youth/women's organization/NGO?
2. If yes, what kind of activities are you involved with?
3. What do you feel/ think of the unrest and insurgency problem in the state?
4. Do you think law and order is a problem in Assam?
5. What do you think of the concept "*Swadhin Asom*"?
6. Do you support or believe the concept of "*Swadhin Asom*"?
7. If yes, please justify?
8. If no, Please justify?

III.

1. How do you look at the future of Assam?
2. What do you think of ULFA, which is going strong despite counter-insurgency in the state?
3. Do you think it has a popular mass support?
4. If yes, why do you think so?
5. If no, why do you think so?
6. What do you think ULFA needs to do now?
7. What do you think Government needs to do now to solve the insurgency problem in Assam?

For **Local Media**

1. Do you think local and regional media has a special role to play?
2. What do you think of your role in this context?
3. What is your view on Arms Forces Special Power Act?

Comment:

ANNEXURE II

Interview Schedule for All Assam Students Union

I.

1. Name:	2. Age:
3. Sex:	4. Occupation:
5. Religion:	6. Caste:

II.

1. How long have you been involved with AASU?
2. What are the activities you are involved with?

   a) Educational b) Social c) Cultural d) Activism
3. How is your organization sustaining?
4. What do you feel/ think of the insurgency problem in the state?
5. Do you think law and order is a problem in the state?
6. What do you think of the concept *"Swadhin Asom"*?
7. Do you support or believe the concept of *"Swadhin Asom"*?

   a) If yes, please justify

   b) If no, please justify

III.

1. How do you look at the future of the state?
2. What are the challenges according to you Assam will face in the coming years?

3. From the past we assume that ULFA came into existence from AASU, what are your comments in this regard?
4. Does AASU support any of ULFA's ideologies?
   a) If yes, please elaborate
   b) If no, please elaborate
5. Why do you think ULFA is still sustaining?
6. Is AASU somehow helping ULFA to sustain?
7. Do you think ULFA has a popular mass support now?
8. If yes, please justify
9. If no, please justify
10. How do you suggest to tackle the insurgency problem in the state?
11. What is the role of ASSU in this context?
12. What is your view on Arms Forces Special Power Act?

ANNEXURE III

Map of Northeast India with Boundaries of the Neighbouring Countries

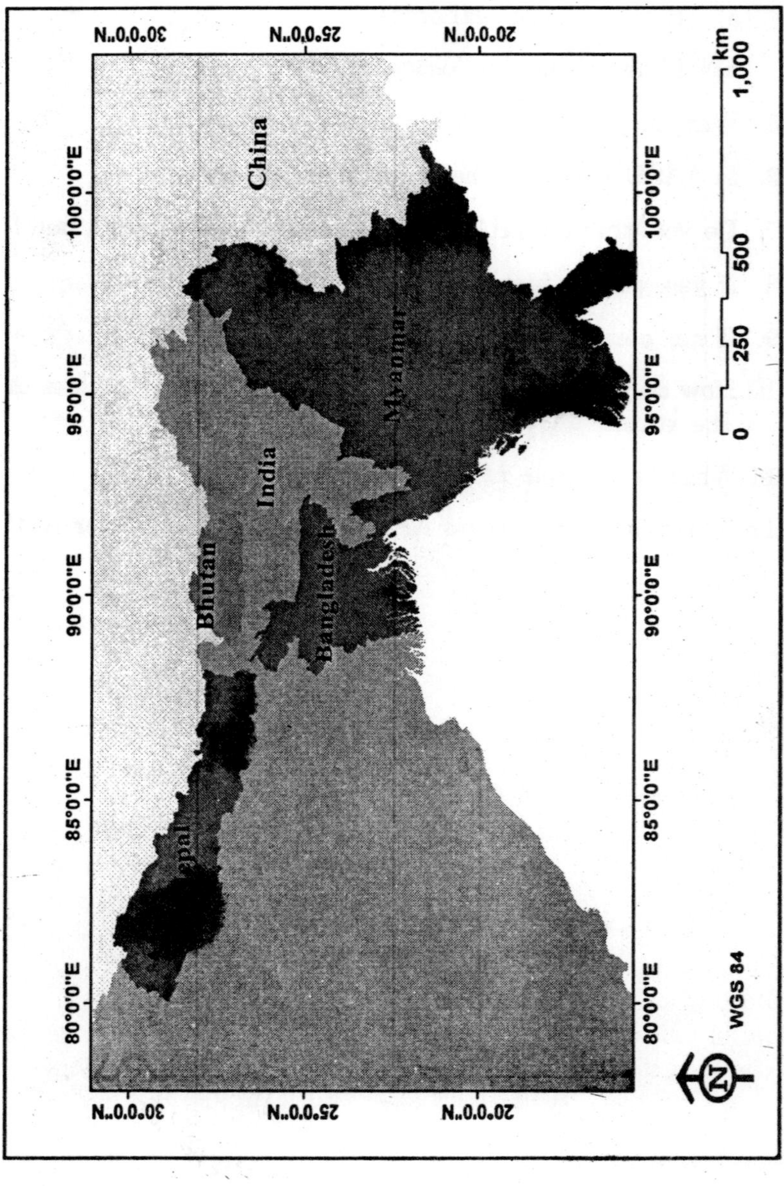

ANNEXURE IV

Map of the Seven States of Northeast India

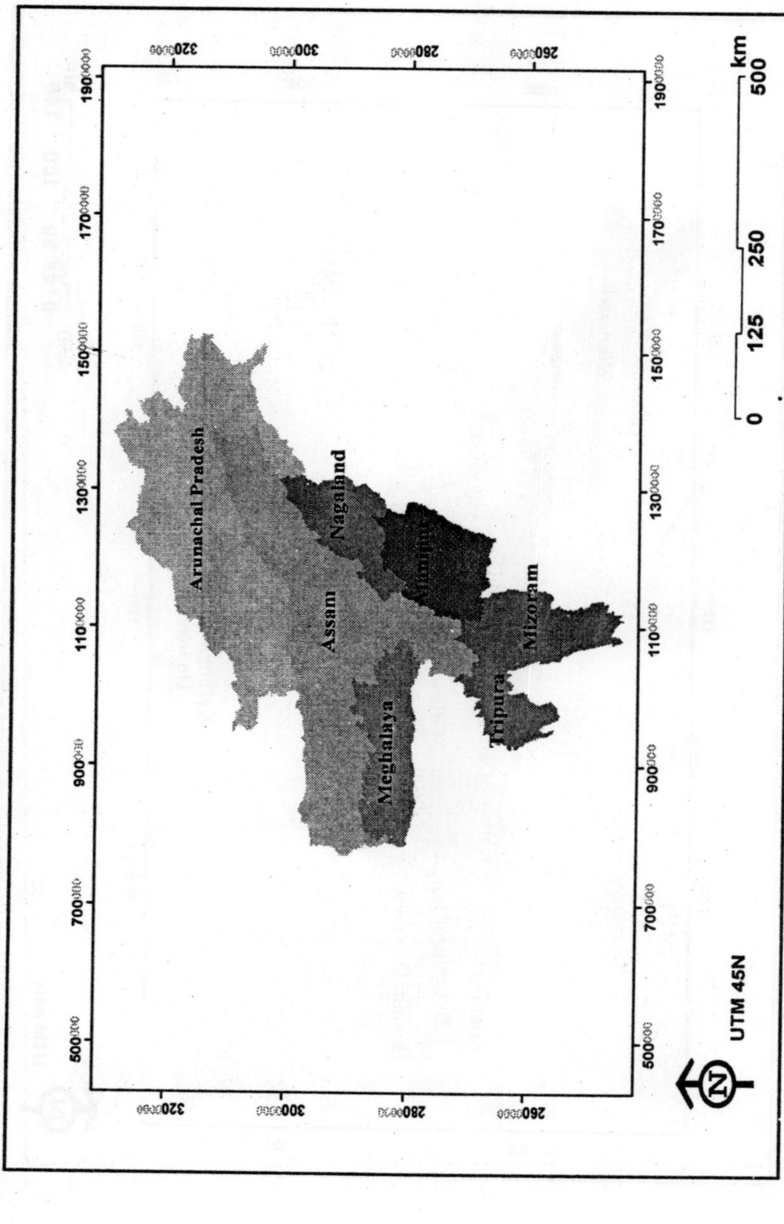

ANNEXURE V

Map of Assam showing the District Boundaries

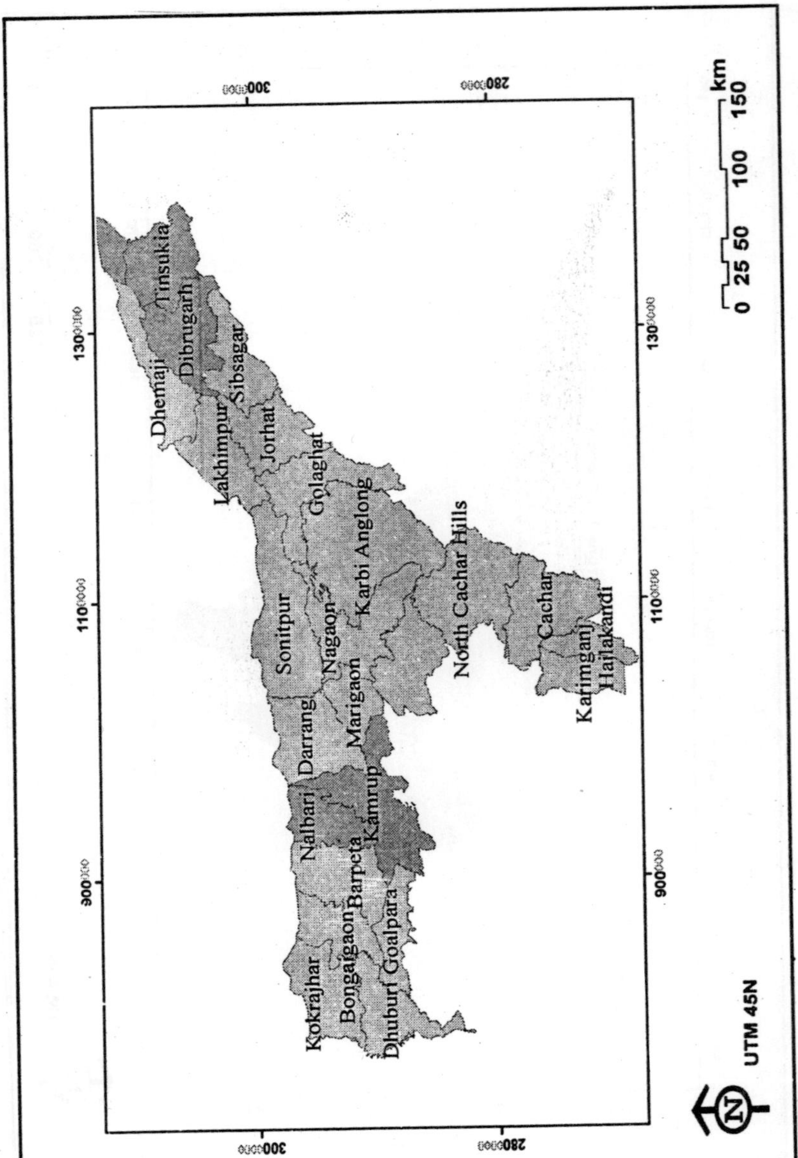

Index

□□□